Aspects of
MODERN ARCHITECTURE

COOP HIMMELBLAU AND HANS HOLLEIN, ENTRY FOR THE EXPO 1995, VIENNA, A SCHEME WHICH DECLARES THE INTENT OF AUSTRIA AND HUNGARY TO CO-HOST A WORLD'S FAIR. THE WINNING ENTRY WAS BY SEPP FRANK AND WILL BE FEATURED IN A FUTURE ISSUE.

Architectural Design

Edited by Andreas C Papadakis

Aspects of
MODERN ARCHITECTURE

OPPOSITE: JEAN ROBERT MAZAUD, SAINT-OUEN II PLANT, FRANCE, SEE PP 80-81
ABOVE: HARRY REIJNDERS, SLOTERDIJK RAILWAY STATION, AMSTERDAM, SEE PP 82-83

ACADEMY EDITIONS • LONDON

Acknowledgements

We are especially grateful to Odile Decq for preparing the feature on *Young French Architecture*
The feature *Information, The 'Gothic Solution'* is reproduced from the recent publication by Martin Pawley,
Theory and Design in the Second Machine Age, published by Basil Blackwell at £27.50,
and is included here with the permission of the publishers
The interview with Zoe Zenghelis was conducted by Vivian Constantinopoulos

Photographs

All photographs supplied by the architects and authors. Credits are as follows:
Title Page Jan Derwig; *Inside Back Cover* illustration courtesy of ZKM, Karlsruhe, supplied by Mediagramm; *Back Cover* Ansai; *pp 54-65* Alberto Piovano; *pp 68-69* Mario Pignata-Monti & Luc Buegly, Archipress; *pp 70-73* Stéphane Couturier, Archipress; *pp 74, 76-77* Jean-Marie Monthiers; *pp 78-79* Nicolas Borel; *pp82-89* Jan Derwig & Sybolt Voeten

PETER PRAN-ELLERBE BECKET, RIKSHOSPITAL, OSLO

EDITOR
Dr Andreas C Papadakis

EDITORIAL OFFICES: 42 LEINSTER GARDENS, LONDON W2 3AN TELEPHONE: 071-402 2141
CONSULTANTS: Catherine Cooke, Dennis Crompton, Terry Farrell, Kenneth Frampton, Charles Jencks,
Heinrich Klotz, Leon Krier, Robert Maxwell, Demetri Porphyrios, Colin Rowe, Derek Walker.
EDITORIAL TEAM: Maggie Toy (House Editor), James Steele (Senior Editor), Vivian Constantinopoulos, Helen Castle
DESIGNED BY: Andrea Bettella, Mario Bettella SUBSCRIPTIONS MANAGER: Mira Joka

First published in Great Britain in 1991 by *Architectural Design*
an imprint of the
ACADEMY GROUP LTD, 7 HOLLAND STREET, LONDON W8 4NA
ISBN: 1-85490-102-8 (UK)

Architectural Design Profile 90 is published as part of *Architectural Design* Vol 61 3-4/1991
Published in the United States of America by
ST MARTIN'S PRESS, 175 FIFTH AVENUE, NEW YORK 10010
ISBN: 0-312-06705-4 (USA)

Printed and bound in Singapore

PETER PRAN-ELLERBE BECKET, RIKSHOSPITAL, OSLO

Contents

Architectural Design Profile No 90

Aspects of
MODERN ARCHITECTURE

KENNETH POWELL
MAPPING THE MODERN

Environmentally and socially responsible; humanistic rather than mechanistic; sensual rather than intellectual; abandoning pretences at 'functionalism' in favour of the dramatic, the evocative, even the fantastic and the seemingly irrational; small-scale and regional rather than universal; pursuing interculturalism (as defined by Kurokawa) rather than internationalism – such is the alleged character of the New Modernism.

Itsuko Hasegawa preaches and practises an architecture – in the extraordinary context of contemporary Japan – which is (in her words) 'responsive to the ecosystem since all human existence is ultimately encompassed by nature'. Abandoning the facile universalism of the old Modernism, Hasegawa is brave enough to talk – as she frequently does – about 'feminine' qualities in architecture. Probably the most significant woman architect practising today, she has created a fantastic, artificial world in the Shonandai Cultural Centre, a place where trees, caves and flowers are made of metal. The hanging garden in her Nagoya Pavilion is meant to create a symbiotic relationship with nature. These gardens are man-made, colourless, unchanging – the relationship with nature comes from the sky and the action of light on materials. A 'new kind of nature'? Or a distorted and even obscene imitation of the real world? The virtue of Hasegawa's work lies in its ruthless attack on technological certainties and its rejection of simple-minded consumerism. Yet, as Botond Bognar all but concedes, Hasegawa could equally create the biggest and best (or worst) Disneyworld ever seen. Her architecture has immense potential for fine-grained, humane placemaking – as her houses powerfully underline. Equally, its beguiling artificiality could point the way to an unstructured nihilism which is a commentary on the worst traits of late 20th-century Japanese society. Yet it is impossible to deny that the work is riveting and a necessary corrective to the cool monumentalism of other Japanese designers.

The relative sobriety of recent French architecture leaves much of it curiously suspended in time and uncertain in spirit. Monumentalism – of a joyless sort – still persists in many circles in France. As a response to it, the small-scale work of some younger French architects is refreshingly irresponsible and anarchic. That energy can be harmlessly dispersed in the styling of the restaurant, the boutique, the night-club. Brunet & Saunier's tower house is something more significant: a superficially logical, ultimately perverse approach to house extension – a prison for the aspiring scholar.

If there is a New Modern spirit at large, with some of the characteristics I referred to earlier, it cannot find full expression in the one-off house, the music store, or the cultural centre. Traditional Modernist planning and social dogmas may be discredited but the issue of the 'public domain' remains. How far can public architecture provide a forum for innovation and experiment? How can public buildings preach unpredictablitity and uncertainty in a society looking for a reaffirmation of lost certainties? Far from being questioning, transient, they need to imply durability and security.

In Britain, a new generation of transport buildings, including Nicholas Grimshaw's Channel Tunnel terminal, Foster's Stansted Airport and some of the smaller railway stations commissioned by Jane Priestman's regime at BR appeals to Victorian virtues: calm, solidity and reliability. They are straightforward, only indirectly referential – a preserve of old values?

The astonishing station building programme pursued by the state railways in the Netherlands is based on different premises. The station, they suggest, is not merely a mechanically efficient place of transit but rather a social and cultural centre. Brightly coloured, illuminated by night, screaming their presence across the flat urban landscape of Holland, they defy the sensible Dutch to be so insane, so irresponsible as to even consider driving their cars into the city. Visit the station – even think of taking a train . . . Inspiration comes from a promiscuous variety of sources – the Pompidou Centre, Rietveld's Schroeder House, even, one feels, Legoland. Where is the rationale behind it all? Have the Dutch abandoned their legendary good sense – and taste? It would not happen in Britain, nor in France.

Taste, sense, responsibility – how do these virtues rate amidst an architectural revolution where past values are being rubbished? A few weeks ago I heard Peter Eisenman describing Disneyworld as 'the ultimate mediated environment . . . a particular extreme of non-reality' and wasn't quite sure whether that description implied approval or condemnation. Or whether to introduce values into the discussion at all was appropriate.

Eisenman has been identified with a crusade against the predictable and the 'homogeneous'. The New Modernism, for all its emphasis on a certain folksiness and self-conscious artiness, rejects codified values in favour of a New Age individualism; in effect, an *ad hoc* existentialism which is fuelled by the Deconstructivists.

My concern, despite all the joyfulness, the invention, the artifice seen in this issue is for the city and for urban values. In the end, Hasegawa's pursuit of nature through architecture may be at the expense of the social fabric which makes life either fulfilling or unbearable. New Modernism urgently needs a philosophy of urbanism.

Kenneth Powell is Correspondent for *The Daily Telegraph*, and member of the Academy Forum Council
OPPOSITE: Itsuko Hasegawa, Shonandai Cultural Centre, Fujisawa

STEPHEN PERRELLA

ANTERIOR DIAGRAMMATICS, WRITING WEAK ARCHITECTURE

Stephen Perrella is a New York correspondent for Architectural Design. *He is an architect and editor of the monthly publication* NEWSLINE *at Columbia University Graduate School of Architecture, Planning and Preservation.*

Liz Diller and Ricardo Scofidio, performance/lecture diagrammatic image

This essay concerns mapping contemporary architectural theory. While only explored here in a cursory fashion, the use of a map for this task contains elements necessary to access certain features of a variety of contemporary theory-practices. This textual interrogation of the word/text *map* yields a terrain inscribed with historical and philosophical assumptions operating in everyday circumstances involving the spoken and written, objects and images. Further scrutiny of these historically derived categories elicits questions concerning the role played by models and paradigms in architectural theory and how metaphysics institutionalises relations between representation and thought. The analysis broaches the issue of how science and philosophy have, historically, established models of unity which have then been transferred to the realm of architectural theory, and which underlie all architecture. This investigation suggests that a certain sensibility in contemporary theory-practices, parallel to and in resonance with the tradition of continental philosophy, enables interrogation of the history of metaphysics as it has influenced architectural history. This interrogation transforms the role models or paradigms play in formulating meaning in architecture: models here are used in a weaker manner, as diagrams. New possibilities for considering space and time result from this change in relations between object and theory: architecture without metaphysics becomes diagrammatic, and what results may be considered a writing of weak architecture.

Mapping Architectural Theory

In cultural theory, maps have been projected to discern the contents and boundaries of various philosophical and cultural traditions. This essay is not a simple attempt to illustrate certain tendencies in architectural theory but instead asks the question: What does any attempt to map already presuppose? The essay will not map a past history but rather will allow history to speak *through* the analysis. Maps are used as references establishing authoritarian interstices that anticipate a time in which movement is co-ordinated by a pre-established system of references. Graphic maps, in concert with texts, conspire to authorise trajectories and locate positions. However, because of what mapping already presupposes – because of the manner in which a map issues forth what is being represented – mapping a theoretical discourse should trigger suspicion. The map is not innocent. A graphic map facilitating direction and location will not be provided here; instead the spatial and temporal dimensions of language and text will be used as a means to investigate theory. This interrogation of a cartography of architectural theory constitutes a strategy not to repress certain theoretical traditions but to elicit, at least initially, vulgar distinctions.

Map?

A map (noun form) can help to situate the framework of a theory and locate categorical cultural histories that configure relations between theoretical models and objects, whereas the verb *to map* slips off somewhat disruptively into the gap between theory and its object. Theory about architecture that presupposes remaining in reference to its object must establish correspondence with a system of meaning. This, generally speaking, is a metaphysical operation. The elements used to fix boundaries, ideas and other characteristics of foundational thought operating in architecture in fact separate theory from its objects. Rational architectural theory and practice maintain a similar assumption about the normative logic of mapping. But today there also exist theory-practices only accessed through a map that weaves through a system of differences rather than representation. Reading the word *map* as a noun and as a verb entails an inherent slippage between two states. In one, meaning is a medium for truth; in the other, meaning is put at risk. One is foundational, one non-foundational; one wants to be located, and one resonates as conditions for a map of possibilities. This vulgar distinction already divides the possible discourses of contemporary architectural theory, establishing a map with clear boundaries. This boundary, however vulgar, anticipates an anterior dimension in theory which this essay will struggle to valorise. In so doing, it may repress the historical and philosophical dimensions possible in a more subtle reading of a map of cultural history – but no study can fully cover all theory.

Map/p(ing)

The distinctions inscribed in the word *map* may be indexed by writing it as map/p(ing). The verb form signals a fault line in the map of theory. The implications of the fault bear on the dichotomy between theory and practice, marking the opening of a space anterior to architecture in its everyday appearance. The theory-scape fictionalised in this anterior space-time entails interwoven vagaries of historicity and the various traditions at work in contemporary culture. This geography, however, simultaneously surrenders itself by implication in the constituting of such a terrain. In part, the criteria for this sense of mapping, the 'map' itself, is understood as simultaneously theoretical because of what it issues forth by way of access to other theories. At the same time this mapping serves as a representation traversing a discourse, it also endeavours to sacrifice its capacity to elicit any truth by positing itself as theory. In this condition of both describing and being theory, the theory of mapping becomes a realm that resonates.

This textual reading limits ethical-political and other horizons that should not be left unconsidered in an investigation of architectural theory. Yet a textual reading of what a map entails affords a glimpse of what will be privileged and cautiously indexed as *anterior*. This essay argues that contemporary theory-practices are not to be perceived via the assumptions inherited intact from contemporary culture but rather via recognition that an/other possibility exists – an anterior possibility. This entails not simply accepting natural perception as a by-product of the metaphysics of presence but developing a mode of approaching thought and work informed by a tradition of interrogating cultural history.

The End of the Metaphysics of Presence/The Anterior Condition

Anterior: [Latin, compar. of ante before – more at ANTE-] 1541 1) A: *situated before or towards the front* B: *situate near or towards the head or part most nearly corresponding to a head. 2) coming before in time or development.*[1]

To rethink the necessity of metaphysics, where words and objects referentially constitute meaning, the attempt is made here to find the always already textual condition of the word/text *map*, even to the extent of avoiding texts referring to images. This redirection opens a space anterior to metaphysics. This positing surrenders authoritative situating by interrogating preconceptions. This involves neither closing down nor distorting what is being discussed but suggests that what is discussed simply does not exist. This exploration of the relationship of a fictional geography and American architectural discourse is a minor plotting, a fictional history. The concern is not to implement or plot the origins of truth of the future theoretical trajectories or historical teleologies but to amplify the characteristics of architectural space-time at the end of metaphysics. What makes architecture and its theorisation anterior involves interrogating the grounds on which a theory of architecture stands. This is the closing of history and the opening of historicity. When Princeton University professor and architectural theorist Mark Wigley, in his article 'The Translation of Architecture: The Product of Babel', writes the programme for an architectural historicity, it is a geographic programme, outlining the geography of an anterior dimension. Wigley explains:

Since there is no safe place to begin, one can only enter the economy and trace its convoluted geometry in order to describe this scene of translation. This can be done by locating that moment in each discourse where the other is made thematic, where the other comes to the surface. The line of argument that surfaces there can then be folded back on the rest of the discourse to locate other layers of relationship. These hidden layers are not simply below the surface. To locate them involves slippage along fault-lines rather than convoluted folds of this surface; it is a matter of following some circular line of inquiry, or circulating within the economy, within the surface itself.[2]

Anteriority generally may be used to characterise work that practises self-scrutiny. We may consider here the second sense of the definition of the word *anterior*: coming before in time or development. The particular sense of 'before' intended here is not a before that may be reached objectively but approaches the sense in which Martin Heidegger discusses history in *What is a Thing*:

The conception of the question 'What is a thing?' as historical is just as far removed from the intention of merely reporting historically about former opinions about the things as it is from the mania for criticising

these opinions and, by adding together what is temporarily correct, from figuring out and offering a new opinion from past opinions. Rather it is a question of setting into motion the original inner happening of this question according to its simplest characteristic moves, which have been arrested in a quiescence. This happening does not lie somewhere aloof from us in the dim and distant past but is here in every proposition and in each everyday opinion, in every approach to things.[3]

The notion of *anteriority* exhibits the capacity to be used generally and textually in various works of continental philosophy. Anterior thought scrutinises the tradition of history based on a foundation. Instead of being simply accepted, an interrogation and transformation occurs such that the ability to operate strictly within the functions of logic is problematised.

Rigorous contemporary architecture may not simply be described as complex or disrupted or radical. The foundation on which radical work sits is constituted culturally. Many figures in the continental tradition concerned with anteriority have investigated the cultural-historical ground thought possible. Anterior architecture can anticipate being apprehended *before* that act of apprehension because it questions the culturally inherited system of apprehension. Scrutinising architecture's historicity has an effect on architecture's capacity to be presented in fullness, full presentness. Such work is of more than shock value. It is the product of thinkers who, suspecting rational history that altered their understanding of traditional history and its products and of how current events undergo this transformation.

Anterior Space-time

How can we come upon something that has prefigured our response, unless what it has prefigured involves our very capacity to figure? Anterior work manages to access what is constitutive of any apprehending by inhabiting tradition. The effect then is of managing to catch a glimpse of our own seeing. Anteriority displaces the sequence of scientific time. Typically, we come upon things armed with specific expectations; if we encounter something unexpected, this norm is disrupted. Anteriority is similar to disruption but continues, whereas simple disruption is no more than a temporary distraction. Anteriority is the possibility of a new space-time, a condition simultaneously at the threshold and the boundaries of what seems most significant in architectural theory. In gaining access to this terrain, replete with gaps and fissures, one gains access to what is already at work in any thought about architecture. Here arises a distinction between theory that presupposes material as the possible ground for theorising architecture and always sets off from that path, and anterior thought which locates its terrain in historicity. Anterior theory can only exist as an operation that works through and with our Western cultural tradition. Philosopher John Rajchman, in 'What's New in Architecture', discusses the space-time of anteriority in terms of an event:

An architecture of the event would be an architecture of this other relation to history: it would 'eventualise' or open up what, in our history or our tradition, presents itself as 'monumental', as what is assumed to be essential and unchangeable, or incapable of a 'rewriting', as what is 'fixed in concrete'. It would, as it were, interrupt or dislocate what the *demiurgos* or architect of History would be thought to have con-

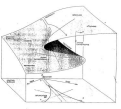

Peter Eisenman Architects, Catastrophe theory model, taken from a recent issue of Scientific American

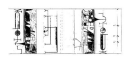

Jeffrey Kipnis and Stephen Perrella, Angelic Wall-Column, 1990, elevation. Wall-Column design for SoHo Art Gallery. Tectonic use of angelic signatures (recently demolished).

Sunday	*Monday*
Michaēl	Gabriel
⚫	☽
name of the 4.*th Kaavu*	*name of the* 1.*st Kaavu*
Machen.	Shamain.

'Near image' diagrams used in Kipnis/Perrella Gallery collaboration

Vitruvian Man

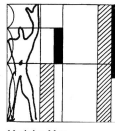

Modulor Man

Stephen Perrella and Jeffrey Kipnis, Choragic Monument Competition, The Architectural League, New York, summer 1990 collaboration diagram for architecture of the new millennium

structed once and for all in conformity with a given plan, programme or model. It would, says Derrida, *s'explique avec l'événement*, a way of spacing that gives its place to the event.[4]

Engaging an anterior condition involves tracing the history of developments between science and philosophy and the impact of their interwoven history on architectural theory. For the purposes of this essay, it is not critical to examine such a tracing, although such an analysis needs to be done repeatedly. Architectural theorists have recently identified history as a space for interrogation. In his book of aphorisms, *In The Manor of Nietzsche: Aphorisms around and about Architecture*,[5] Jeffrey Kipnis, professor of architecture at Ohio State University, identifies characteristics of architectural history that render the rational basis of history suspect. In the first statement notice that Kipnis cites the role played by models:

Aphorism No 8. Both architectural history and theory continue to ground their propositions in examples. Yet, the problem with 'examples' is that there is always an examination of the example available which demonstrates that it exemplifies a contradiction to the very precept for which it is taken to stand.

Aphorism No 9. The history of architecture is not the chronology of architectural form but the genealogy of architectural will.

Aphorism No 10. It cannot be ignored, however, that at a moment and as a movement in the genealogy, the architectural will characterised architectural history as a chronology of form.

Aphorism No 11. The principle of a counter-history: A period of architecture ends when style stresses the importance of man. A new period begins when style causes stress to the 'importance' of 'man'.

Mark Wigley has also contributed to the notion of an anterior history of architecture. In his catalogue introduction to the 1988 Deconstructivist architecture exhibition at The Museum of Modern Art, Wigley states:

The architect has always dreamed of pure form, of producing objects from which all instability and disorder have been excluded. Buildings are constructed by taking simple geometric forms – cubes, cylinders, spheres, cones, pyramids and so on – and combining them into stable ensembles, following compositional rules which prevent any one form from conflicting with another. No form is permitted to distort another; all potential conflict is resolved. The forms contribute harmoniously to a unified whole. This constant geometric structure becomes the physical structure of the building: its formal purity is seen as guaranteeing structural stability.[6]

Wigley's discussion indicates the relationship between philosophy and architecture inasmuch as forms can exist in pure thought. Plato, a philosopher, established the terrain of pure thought, but further scrutiny may reveal the dimensions that science has played in affording models for pure thought, ideals from which all objects would reference. Both Kipnis and Wigley are keenly aware of the manner in which history has been shaped. Both call, in their respective agendas, for an interrogation of and a new attitude towards history. One possible vector through the various underlying paradigms in architecture that encompasses the relation between philosophy and science is presented in Alberto Pérez-Gómez's *Architecture and the Crisis of Modern Science*.[7] The author analyses the relationship between geometry and culture, and his discussion

of the source of architectural paradigms implicates philosophy. Pérez-Gómez questions the way in which geometry effects meaning in architecture. Although his argument reflects a nostalgia for the metaphysical relations immanent in geometry before certain scientific revolutions, his work is useful inasmuch as it affords a history of architecture's involvement with models. We may notice in Pérez-Gómez's comments the philosophical/scientific interrelations in architectural theory: 'The Platonic dimension of Galileo's scientific revolution eventually became the main source of technology's dominance in architecture.'[8] Pérez-Gómez's reading of history marks clear distinctions between graphically constituted models and the theories inscribed in architecture. One brief interjection articulates the interrelations of historical, material and geometric issues: Jacques Derrida's critique of historical reason in the introduction to Edmund Husserl's *The Origin of Geometry* identifies how the 'historicity of ideal object' is established.

In general terms, *ideal objects* for Husserl are spiritual formations which have their origin in human activity and especially in human thought, and not in nature. Thus, already constituted spiritual objects cannot be sensibly perceived either. They are understood in their sense-content and are optimally rethought in their original meaning. Compared with natural objects which are located in objective space and time and can only be perceived perspectively, ideal objects have the decisive advantage of being universally available and consequently strictly objective. Such ideal objects are secure from the chances and changes of nature and cannot be claimed as a private possession by any individual subject. This immutability or 'omnitemporality' . . . this universality and objectivity make the ideal object into the 'absolute model' for any object whatever.[9]

Derrida's interest in Husserl's assumption about ideal objects focuses on problematising the ideas (*eidos*) on which the history of metaphysics depends. The map of the metaphysician relies upon a system in which representations – verbal or graphic, objects or texts – corresponds to particular referents. An overarching structure ensures the correspondence of such relations, a structure that results from a history in which philosophy and science have conspired towards establishing and maintaining coherence. Science has, especially since the Renaissance, issued forth models as explanations for physical phenomena. These models have always been attempts at complete and coherent explanations. Since Aristotle, philosophy has built metaphysical assumptions into science. The models of science and philosophy have served as diagrams informing all other disciplines, and the history of architectural theory is replete with such models.

The relationship between geometry, science, philosophy and architecture currently amounts to a crisis of representation. In Mark Wigley's unpublished doctoral dissertation, *Jacques Derrida and Architecture: The Deconstructive Possibilities of Architectural Discourse*, the author sorts through the crisis of representation in a historical account of the interrelations laid out by Pérez-Gómez. Wigley traces a history in which architecture has played a role, enabling the power relations and delusions of wholeness to which contemporary culture agrees contractually. (Wigley's discourse is one of the few in architectural thought to address adequately the gap between architecture and philosophy.) In subsequent texts, greater attention will be paid to what

10

Wigley has already negotiated, but here we may glean from a few comments from Wigley regarding his reading of the crisis of representation that allude to the depth and complexity of the issue:

> Pérez-Gómez repeatedly describes the crisis of modern architecture in terms of a degeneration from symbols to signs. This degeneration was made possible by a transformation in the status of drawing whereby '. . . represented images lost their symbolic dimension and became prosaic signs of material reality.' In modern theory, the drawing is but a 'vehicle' employed in the construction of a project, a sign '. . . devoid of value in itself.' This transformation was effected by new projective geometries which displaced the presentational Euclidean geometry and reversed the traditional privileging of presentation over representation: 'Reality as presence and reality as appearance were not only intentionally disjoined, but the primacy of undistorted presence was replaced by the primacy of distorted appearance.' Geometrical forms '. . . were uprooted from. . . their traditional values.' The transformation of architectural theory from metaphysical justification to technological instrument is, therefore, a degeneration from symbol to sign, presentation to representation.[10]

The issue to which the above text only alludes involves the complex history in which the graphic/image/diagram *qua* representation has become entangled in the realm of metaphysics.

From Wigley's investigation, we shift to Kipnis, who has also established the impetus and basis for a discussion involving paradigms in a text for a competition done in collaboration with myself. The panel of this (last place) entry for the Choragic Competition sponsored by the Architectural League in New York City explicates specific models as they have influenced architectural meaning. The panel reads:

> A Diagram for Other Architectures: Since the Renaissance the ideology, the philosophy and the aesthetics of the two major bodies of architectural thought have been captured in two respective diagrams, Leonardo da Vinci's Vitruvian Man and Le Corbusier's Modulor. A close reading of these two diagrams individually and comparatively yields the entire system of similarities and differences encompassed in the relationship between classical and modern architecture. Though chronologically these diagrams emerged after the beginnings of the architecture which they inscribe, in a certain sense, nevertheless, each of them can be understood to have governed their respective architectures. The legacy of the 20th century for design is a compelling mandate to pursue and articulate Other Architectures.

Kipnis describes the Vitruvian Man as a marrying of divine geometry to divine man, evidencing dominant models in architecture from the Renaissance to the modern. The Modulor dissolves the unified cosmology of the prior diagram into the characteristic Western mind/body duality, evidencing a split between the body and its theorisation. All of the characteristics attributed to this figure are Cartesian/Kantian epistemological rather than classical ontological terms. In each case, a pre-established cosmology or extension of geometrical proportions renders these models references to which a system of metaphysical relations establishes correspondence. Kipnis, in partnership with Bahram Shirdel and Andrew Zago, currently

summarises these operations by differentiating 'pattern book' methodology in which Vitruvian man is an example of the underlying assumption of classical architecture and 'analysis synthesis' methodology effected through the use of the Corbusian Modulor. In both cases man is the measure of built things, and certain systems of referentiality are maintained.

What would happen if these models were subjected to a history of metaphysics that results in its own metaphysical exhaustion? What would be the status of these models if metaphysics was somehow circumvented? Derrida's reading of Husserl's *The Origins of Geometry* is useful inasmuch as it, as does all of Derrida's work, problematises metaphysics. Derrida instigates an interrogation of our cultural habits regarding the spoken and the textual such that the text is a supplement to language. Indeed, he finds this to be the case in a number of significant philosophical works since the beginning of Western thought. Derrida's research argues that spoken language is privileged over writing. He also points out the resonating condition between the textual and the phonetic: sometimes textual, sometimes phonetic, the in-between state of meaning renders it undecidable. Meaning is neither in the text nor associated with the speaking subject; instead it is adrift in a fluctuating state in a system of differences that Derrida argues is the condition for the possibility of meaning. Derrida has invented devices that effect and elicit a disruption of the dream of metaphysics, including grafting, the *pharmakon, différance* and the trace.

Although architecture has adopted the strategies of deconstruction, what Derrida has been thought not to have accounted for is the object. This became evident to architect Peter Eisenman and to theorists Kipnis and Wigley when Derrida became directly involved in Bernard Tschumi's 1988 La Villette project. Derrida manifested what appeared to be humanist concerns: where people would sit and where trees would be planted. (There is much more to be said about Derrida's involvement with architecture, particularly regarding Tschumi's work, but this would entail an entirely different path for the essay.) Eisenman, Kipnis and Wigley, however, realised that the context of philosophy (language and text) was not exactly the same as that of architecture. Kipnis is currently writing a detailed account of the collaboration entitled *A Choral Work*. Wigley, in *The Pratt Journal of Architecture, Vol 2: Form, Being, Absence*[11] (1988) called for an 'Architectural Displacement of Philosophy.' Deconstruction, after 25 years of existence, had finally arrived in the discipline of architecture. Architecture, as delineated by Kant in his third critique, is the lowest form of the arts. Wigley argued that when deconstruction arrived on the scene of architecture – its last stop – deconstruction would have to change. This is where the most rigorous thought in architectural theory is being done. In a recent series of lectures at Columbia University, Eisenman noted that architecture is a non-dialogic third, a term in excess of the binary oppositions of Derrida's deconstruction of the spoken and written. Eisenman claimed that this was to be construed as architecture's resistance to deconstruction. Indeed, the possibility of the end of metaphysics in architecture must be further interrogated.

The correspondence between theory and its object in architecture currently privileges the object, but the relation between the model and the object has historically enabled understanding in theory. A transformation of the model generates a diagram, a system of relational trajectories that

Shirdel, Zago, Kipnis, La Place Jacques Cartier, Montreal, 1990-2000, International Competition in Urban Design and Urban Planning, May 1990. Projection of near image (form-shape, shift) onto competition context.

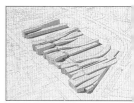

Peter Eisenman, Columbus Convention Center, Ohio

Studio Asymptote (Hani Rashid and Lisanne Coture), 'Nebula configuration: breathing mode/Zero sound – first sound', Bay-Adelaide Public Art Competition, Toronto, winning entry, 1991-92. Slated for construction in 1992.

Hiroshi Maruyama, House for a Craftsman, 1990, diagram

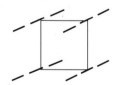

El Lissitzky diagrams, K und pan Geometry, El Lissitzky, MIT Press, Cambridge, 1970

cohere as a working explanation for some object. In the attempt to map these developments, it became evident that one issue had yet to be addressed. Further inquiry may elaborate the transformation of metaphysical systems of thought in contemporary theory-practices. Whereas the textual, the phonetic, the graphic and the object status of a map are the conditions for a map of possibilities, our cultural tendencies are such that each of these categories is always in a fixed correspondence to a prescribed reference or model: the text refers to the alphabet, the phonetic refers to a shared cultural language system and the object refers to a metaphysical theory. Derrida, in the context of philosophy, dealt with the spoken and written; Eisenman, Kipnis and Wigley raised the issue of the object; what does not seem accounted for is the *graphic* condition.

Architectural theorist Catherine Ingraham, under the rubric of the 'Burdens of Linearity,' has pursued the implications of this 'missing' condition. Ingraham describes her theory as a departure from Derrida's chapter 'Of Grammatology as a Positive Science,' which led her to consider the apparatus (a photocopying machine) as a framing instrument. Her engaging work warrants attention, especially her introduction to the issue of technicity. There would seem to be another route in accounting for a deconstruction of the graphic condition, the image without metaphysics.

Kipnis should be credited for making it possible to think through the graphic/image issue in architectural theory. In his work as a partner in the firm Shirdel, Zago, Kipnis, he argues that 'shape is all there is'. Kipnis was perhaps the first to notice the diagrammatic implications available through a deconstruction of the history of architectural theory. He and his partners' work has begun to investigate the implications of the image in architectural displacement. This is not to say that other deconstructivists like Tschumi, Eisenman and Libeskind do not consider the graphic condition of their work. Rather, the specificity that Kipnis gives the graphic as a primary displacing mechanism may be called the diagrammatic.

Anterior Diagrams, Writing Weak Architecture: Map/p(ing) Space-time

At the end of the space-time of this woven geography is Derrida, who gave the final clue to the problematics of the missing graphic condition:

> Writing is no longer only the word and mnemotechnical aid to a truth whose own being-sense would dispense with all writing-down. The possibility or necessity of being incarnated in a graphic sign is no longer simply extrinsic and factual in comparison with ideal objectivity: it is the *sine qua non* condition of Objectivity's internal completion. . . . The act of writing is the highest possibility of all 'constitution'.[12]

Contemporary architecture, which sets up a possible space for anteriority through which weak architecture may be written, is initiated by displacing paradigms. Throughout the history of thought and architecture form-generators have determined architecture's measure. Anterior architecture has not done away with the paradigm but in using this programmatic model differently transforms it. The paradigms now disrupt the coherence of form to weaken it. If we consider architecture as writing at the end of metaphysics, then all of the possible conditions hitherto chained to truth and metaphysics will be in play in a system of difference. This manner of considering what is here called 'writing weak architecture' at least initially accounts for the

problematics in the relationship between architecture and philosophy and their contingent conditions (this will be pursued further elsewhere).

The theorists/practitioners discussed here do not participate in the belief that truth lies in the work. They direct us elsewhere, to the space-time of anteriority. Historically, there has been an interest in establishing an ideal of which architecture would be a manifestation. The architects of anteriority send us in various directions in the alter-terrain of space-time. The work is always already on the way to meaning *something else* – already pointing other.

With this practice of anterior diagrammatics, the habit of history is being broken. Correct history and its various assumptions regarding time and positioning are being rerouted, over and over again. Time is being rerouted – time in terms of reified pasts, presents and futures.

The diagrammatics that have surfaced in this essay are in and of themselves maps of space-time. Each in its own configuration transforms the model/theory correspondence. Each theory/practice for each project is configured diagrammatically. An outcome of this practice is that all that metaphysics holds fixed is transformed, including the body, the subject and any other phenomena invented by this new work.

Shirdel, Zago, Kipnis

In the work presented here, the architects have managed to work without a system of models as well as effecting a transformation using a displacing diagram, the original of which only existed as a projection. Their displacing diagram was made by projecting 'near figure-shapes' onto a context. The resulting architecture derived from that projection.

Studio Asymptote

The diagram submitted by this group was grafted from accelerator particle tracings onto an existing but altered context. In this manner, the designers defeat metaphysical correspondences by fictionalising the context onto which fictional trajectories are grafted.

Peter Eisenman Architects

Eisenman's original displacing diagram was taken from catastrophe theory in physics. Models used in catastrophe theory were grafted onto a network that was then superposed over a normative grid representing a context. Inevitable distortions arose in the transformation of the normative grid.

Hiroshi Maruyama

In Maruyama's project, a chevron diagram was used to transfigure extensions into the space of a volume. The plan and ceiling plan of the volume, which contain metaphysical correspondences, were displaced because the relations of those two unifying planes in architecture were torn apart by the playing out of ambiguities born from the realm of representation in architecture.

Stanley Allen

Models from psychoanalysis have been used by Allen to displace the perspectival and ideational paradigmatic models. The geometrics of the Lacanian model of subject constitution are inherently paradoxical. Allen embeds the Lacanian diagram in his work such that it transforms the manner in which a subject is constituted in space and time.

Diller & Scofidio

Diller & Scofidio are shown diagramming their work in a performance/lecture given at Columbia University. They operate in the language of diagrammatics, but their work clearly manifests the diagrammatics already at work in any given context. They reveal the diagrammatic content and give the diagram form in order to reveal the spatio-political networks at play in establishing power relations.

Bernard Tschumi

The diagrams submitted by Tschumi include a series of early spatial investigations called the 'Screenplays' (1976-82). Each of the Screenplays were conceptual exercises. Film images used for the project were understood as both montages within a sequence and as distortions and transformations – techniques practised by film-makers.

Each Screenplay is 14 x 36 inches and addresses a thematic theoretical exploration. The panel organises representational devices whereby film images generate a matrix for an architecture strategy composed in three strips: the top sequence are film images, the central strip is the mediating device, and the bottom series depicts the architectural derivations. Each film image is analysed and its characteristics are translated in architectural terms. These include: superimposition, repetition, distortion, fade-in and fade-out, and scale disjunctions. In this particular Screenplay, the film images are collectively part of Lotte Eisner's highly regarded book on Expressionist cinema entitled *The Haunted Screen*. All of the architectural drawings generated from the film images have an archetype in common. The transformation from the film image to the architectural image is effected through the mediation of an abstract filtering device. Transformations include: folding and reflection, twisting and distortion, isolation and opposition, framing and madness, repetition, superimposition and scale disjunction.

Kipnis/Perrella

In a collaboration for a gallery design, Kipnis/Perrella used angelic signatures as a tectonic device to effect a displacement of the historical dichotomy between structure-enclosure. In grafting manipulated signatures upon a wall-column detail, the tradition of repressing its condition is problematised effecting a return of the repressed. The sketch-elevation provided attempts to respect the undecidability of this condition.

Bernard Tschumi, 'Screenplay' panel with matrix of three strips

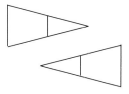

Stanley Allen, diagram of projections (the constructions of the subject), 1991. A diagram of the projection system used to develop designs for a 1990-91 house project in Bucks County, Pennsylvania.

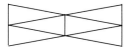

Lacan diagrams (of: object-image-geometral point; point of light-screen-picture; and below: the gaze-image/screen-the subject of representation) from The Four Fundamental Concepts of Psychoanalysis, *Norton Press, New York, 1978*

Notes

1 'Anterior', *Webster's Ninth New Collegiate Dictionary*, Merriam-Webster Inc, Springfield, Massachusetts, 1988.
2 Mark Wigley, 'The Translation of Architecture: The Product of Babel', in 'Deconstruction III', *Architectural Design, Profile No 87*, 1990, p 6.
3 Martin Heidegger, *What is a Thing?*, trans W B Barton, Jr and Vera Deutsch, Regenery/Gateway, Inc, South Bend, Indiana, 1967, p 49.
4 John Rajchman, 'What's New in Architecture', in *Journal of Philosophy and the Visual Arts, 'Philosophy and Architecture'*, ed Andrew Benjamin, Academy Editions, London/St Martins Press, New York, 1990, p 35.
5 Jeffrey Kipnis, *In the Manor of Nietzsche: Aphorisms around and about Architecture*, Calluna Farms Press, 1990.
6 Mark Wigley, *Deconstructivist Architecture,* The Museum of Modern Art, New York, 1988, p 10.
7 Alberto Pérez-Gómez, *Architecture and the Crisis of Modern Science,* MIT Press, Cambridge, Mass, 1983.
8 *Ibid.*
9 Rudolf Bernet, 'On Derrida's "Introduction" to Husserl's *Origin of Geometry*', in *Continental Philosophy II: Derrida and Deconstruction*, ed Hugh J Silverman, Routledge, London and New York, 1989, p 141.
10 Mark Wigley, 'Jacques Derrida and Architecture: The Deconstructive Possibilities of Architectural Discourse', Dissertation, Univ of Auckland 1986, p 13.
11 Mark Wigley, 'The Architectural Displacement of Philosophy,' in *The Pratt Journal of Architecture: Form, Being, Absence*, Rizzoli, New York, 1988, p 86.
12 *Edmund Husserl's Origin of Geometry: An Introduction*, trans John P Leavy, David B Allison (ed), Nicolas Hays, Stony Brook, New York, 1978, p 88.

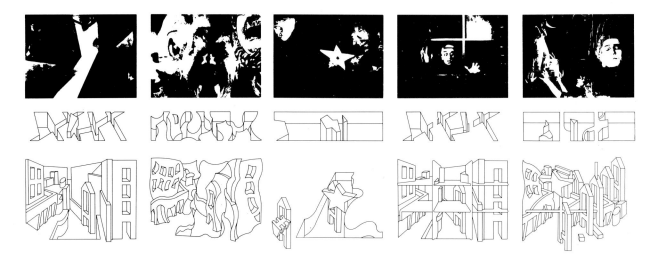

ITSUKO HASEGAWA
ARCHITECTURE AS ANOTHER NATURE
and Recent Projects

The history of humankind is one of continual development and domestication of the earth and destruction of nature. Nature in the wild is not a comfortable place for human beings, and so human beings have created comfortable environments by standing up or adapting to, and transforming nature. The world human beings create, physically speaking, is a mass of artifice, yet deep down it is underpinned by nature. Nature ultimately encompasses all of human existence, and the spaces created by human beings represent an environment, albeit one on a new and different level. The character of that environment is closely tied to the way society and technology have developed historically.

It is not only developments in technology and society that are causing great upheavals but the tempo of those developments. In the past change was gradual and human beings could be sympathetic to, and maintain harmony with nature, but the speed of technological changes today is rapidly bringing about, not just changes to the earth but its destruction. We sense that advanced technology is changing our lives, but we can no longer perceive with any clarity the nature of the technological society in which we live, much less its details.

Today, it is clear that society can no longer simply accept and depend on the modern Western mode of thought. Although those of us living in Asia, with its Buddhist background, ought to be searching for social ideas of our own, we tend to spend our days consuming, distracted by the notion that we can somehow change our lives through material objects. We are without any theory with which to respond to new conditions. As we become materially richer, we begin to sense the superficiality of our lives.

Faced with this situation, people increasingly are focusing on what might be called the primary landscape within themselves, the non-modern as opposed to the modern, the non-urban as opposed to the urban, the non-artistic as opposed to the artistic, the local as opposed to the universal, the indigenous and the ethnic, and the idea of ecology and a relationship of interdependence with nature. Many people are now concerned with the environment, and their concern extends from their immediate surroundings to the globe as a whole. One of my aims is to reconsider architecture of the past, which was adapted to the climate and the land and permitted human coexistence with nature, and to see human beings and architecture as part of the earth's ecosystem. This includes a challenge to propose new design connected with new science and technology.

We also ought to think seriously about restoring architecture to the people in society who use the architecture. It has long been my wish to explore ways of allowing users to participate in a true dialogue with the architect. In designing private houses, I have tried to enter into dialogues with clients and to work jointly with them. Just as I, as an individual, am a part of society, even as I stand outside it, architecture too is a part of the city into which it is introduced. It is important that I do not discard my subjective self, but I must also be willing to look objectively at myself.

These thoughts led me to the conclusion that a building that is used by many people, whatever its scale, ought to be designed not as an isolated work, but as a part of something larger. In other words it must have a quality of urbanity. The city is a changing, multifaceted entity that encompasses even things that are in opposition to it. My second major aim has been to try to eliminate the gap between the community and architecture by taking such an approach to public architecture and to give architecture a new social character.

I believe any new building must make up for the topography and space that is altered because of its introduction and help create a new nature in the place of the one that used to be there. I feel any new building ought to commemorate the nature that had to be destroyed because of it and serve as a means of communicating with nature. The theme of my work is 'architecture as another nature'. We must stop thinking of architecture as something constructed according to reason and distinct from other form of matter. In creating spaces we must recognise that human beings are a part of nature. Architecture must be responsive to the ecosystem as all of human existence is ultimately encompassed by nature.

To put it another way, architecture ought to be such that it allows us to hear the mysterious music of the universe and the rich, yet by no means transparent, world of emotions that have been disregarded by modern rationalism. We need to harness both the spirit of rationalism and the spirit of irrationalism, pay heed to both what is international and what is local, and recognise the nature of contemporary science and technology in trying to create an architecture for the society of the coming era.

The idea of 'architecture as another nature' is one that has met with sympathetic response from citizens, and I believe it can endow architecture with a social character. In the Shonandai Cultural Centre, I created an open, garden-like space at ground level by burying 70% of the total floor area below ground, with much of this underground portion facing sunken gardens, because of this the building is in a certain aspect 'Landscape Architecture'. In effect, a second surface level was created. However, there was opposition among local people who were not accustomed to such underground spaces, and discussions with them about such matters began a whole series of meetings. People have quite different perceptions and tastes. In the process of design, the spaces sometimes reflected the subjective views of the architect and at other times they reflected apposite views. This give and take during the design of the Shonandai Cultural Centre enabled me to think about the relationship between architecture and society.

I have consistently taken an ad hoc approach to architecture rather than an exclusionary stance. Having completed the Shonandai Cultural Centre I realise quite clearly now that I want to create an inclusive architecture that accepts a multiplicity of things rather than an architecture arrived at through reflection and elimination. The idea is to make architecture more realistic through what might be called a 'pop' reasoning that allows for diversity as opposed to a logical system of reasoning that demands extreme concentration. Such an approach represents a shift to a feminist paradigm, in the sense that an attempt is made to raise the consciousness of as many people as possible.

Human beings were born to live in a relationship of interdependence with nature. We are adaptable to change and are physically and spiritually rugged enough to live practically anywhere. I believe this 'feminine' tolerance and consciousness can help to dissolve the system in which we are presently locked and bring about a regeneration.

To sum up, buildings as well as human beings are born of nature, receive their images from nature, and return to a more profound form of life through death and destruction. Another nature will come into being when ideas of the global environment, traditional modes of thought and the 'feminine' concept are married to today's technology. The idea of 'architecture as another nature' is one I will continue to espouse until the arrival of the meta-industrial society and the creation of spaces that are both natural and comfortable to human beings.

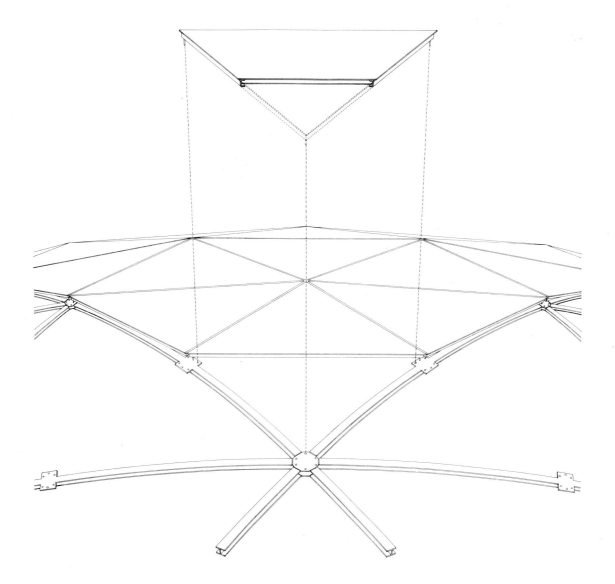

SHONANDAI CULTURAL CENTRE
LEFT: View through perforated metal grids towards
the forecourt
ABOVE: The cultural centre at night

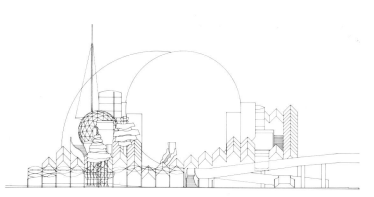

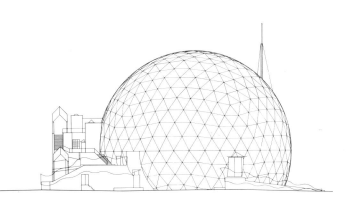

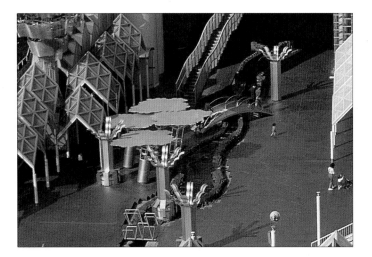

SHONANDAI CULTURAL CENTRE
OPPOSITE PAGE: Details of exterior
LEFT, ABOVE AND BELOW: Exterior views and
south, north and south sectional elevations

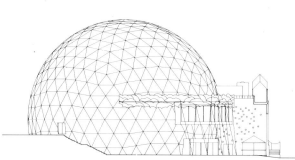

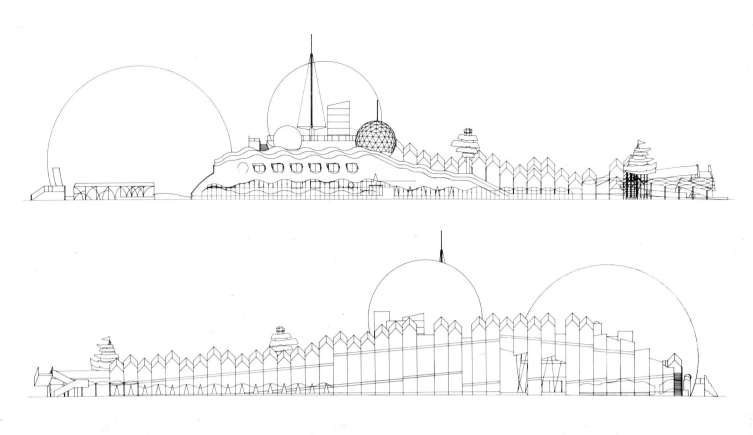

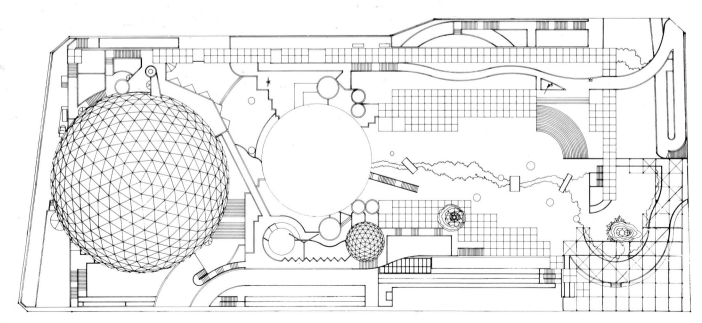

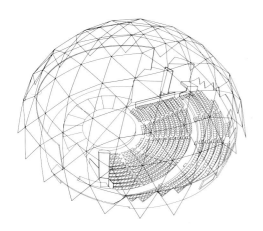

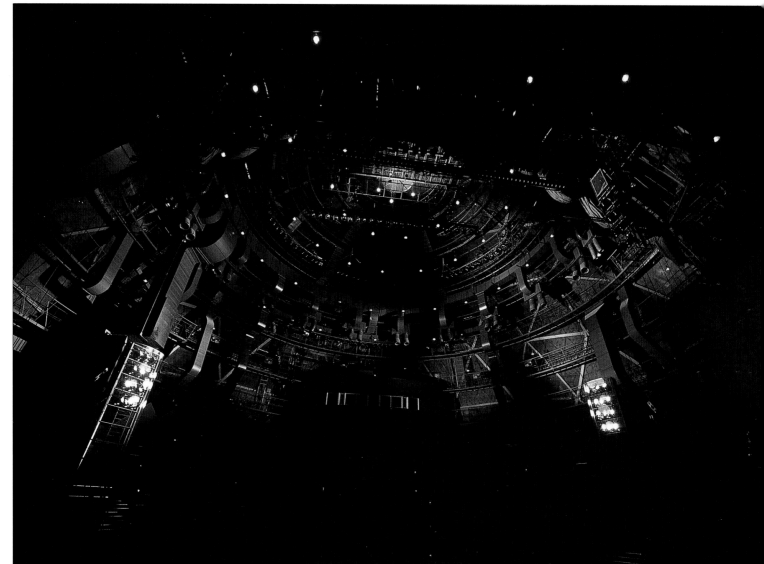

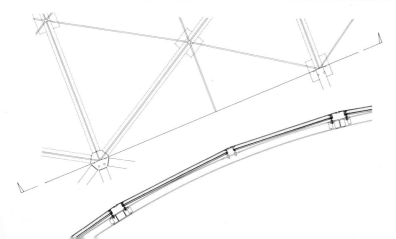

SHONANDAI CULTURAL CENTRE
OPPOSITE PAGE: West and east elevations, details
and roof plan
ABOVE AND LEFT: Diagrammatic axonometric,
interior view and structural detail of auditorium

BIZAN HALL
LEFT: Day and night aerial views
ABOVE: Interior detail and axonometric

KUMAMOTO HOUSE
LEFT: Exterior view
ABOVE AND RIGHT: Elevations, rear view and
plans

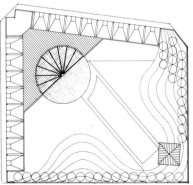
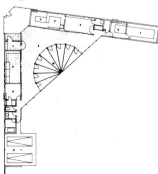

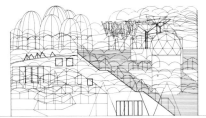

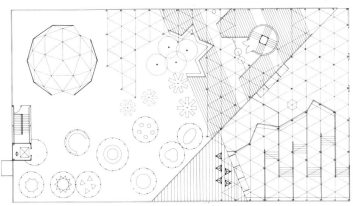

NAGOYA PAVILION
OPPOSITE PAGE: Exterior and forecourt views
LEFT: Bird's-eye view, model and interior view
ABOVE AND BELOW: East elevation, roof plan and south elevation

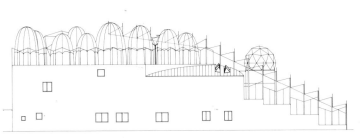

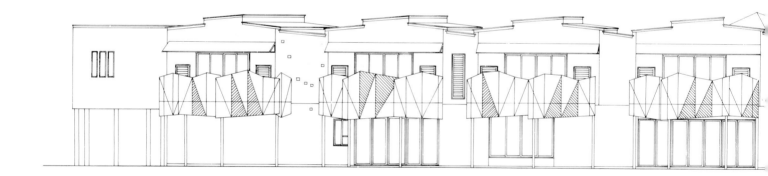

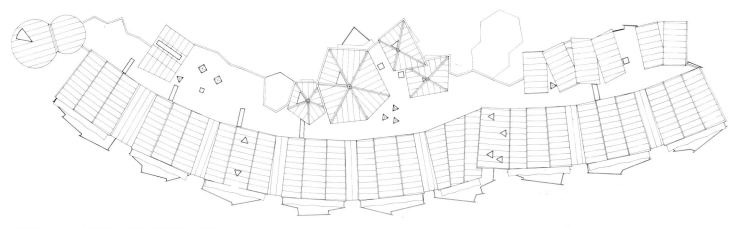

STRESS CARE CENTRE, SHIRANUI HOSPITAL
LEFT AND CENTRE: Riverside elevations
ABOVE: Roof plan
BELOW: Innerside elevation

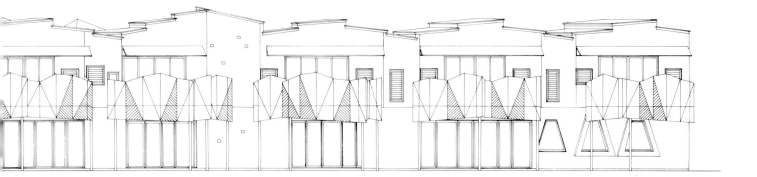

NC HOUSING
ABOVE: *Elevations and exterior views*
RIGHT: *Site plan*

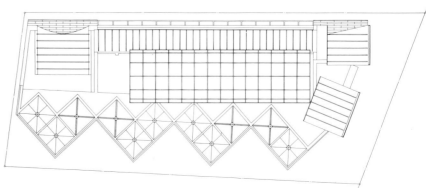

HOUSE AT KUWAHARA
ABOVE: Exterior views
RIGHT: Elevation

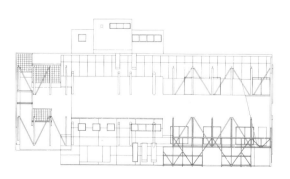

BOTOND BOGNAR
ARCHITECTURE, NATURE & A NEW TECHNOLOGICAL LANDSCAPE
Itsuko Hasegawa's Work in the 80s

'I use architectural and technological details to evoke nature, and natural and cosmic details to evoke architecture.' I Hasegawa [1]

The recently completed Shonandai Cultural Centre (1989) signals both a new highpoint in Hasegawa's career, and perhaps also a turning point in the course of Japanese architecture. The Centre, occupying one large block in the secondary heart of Northern Fujisawa, is the largest work to date by this outstanding designer; it is also one of the first really urban scale, public complexes completed by a new generation of Japanese avant-garde architects – the so called New Wave – who emerged in the 70s and have been coming of age since the mid 80s. Considering the fact that in Japan commissions for large public or governmental projects are customarily awarded to equally large corporate design offices and/or construction companies that turn out 'safe' or reliable but predominantly conservative works reinforcing rather than questioning the status quo of a prevailing rigid modern urbanism, the mere existence of the Centre is already remarkable.

Furthermore, the Shonandai, the result of a winning entry in a nationwide competition, had been designed by one of the handful, and indeed the only really active woman architect in Japan. Through her work, Hasegawa has thus infused a 'feminine voice' in the contemporary Japanese architectural discourse, shaped almost entirely by the representatives of the other gender. Nevertheless, while this 'feminine voice' manifests a unique poetic quality, it bypasses any nostalgic reinterpretation of architecture, the architectural past and the 'lost centre', so common in today's historicist and trivial Post-Modernism.

In the Shonandai, Hasegawa has created an urban 'park' by redefining 'architecture as second nature' so that, while mobilising the 'translucent world of emotions' devoid of the spirit of rationalism, the overall design eschews the sentimental attributes of nature.[2] She introduces nature into her design on two levels: the first, actual nature through the careful yet extensive utilisation of ever changing natural phenomena and the reliance on the evocative but also provocative power of nature; the second, analogical nature, a man-made, industrial/technological, even futuristic construct.

The overall scheme of Hasegawa, quite obviously then, is not an ordinary building that wants to appeal with its overwhelmingly monumental form, as is usual in cases of large public facilities; rather, it is an accumulation of various elements: several spherical volumes of different sizes, light, punched aluminium screens, canopies, series of small, prismatic glass and metallic roofs over an extensive open plaza that includes an amphitheatre, walkways and stairways. The plaza also features some architectural/sculptural devices such as a 'tower of wind and light' and

an artificial 'tree' with a built-in clock. This man-made, high-tech park, contiguous with the surrounding pedestrian areas yet also extended on top of the stepped roofs, is inlaid with green zones of trees, bushes, etc, which interweave with the whole complex in and out. Since the majority of this first level is devoted to outside leisure activities – playing, gathering, strolling – the more specific functions of the centre are arranged in either the spherical structures or are set underground. The globes house theatres and galleries, while the first basement level accommodates offices, lounges, practice rooms, an exhibition hall for children, etc, that all face small sunken gardens; parking and additional machinery rooms are on the second basement level.

Since the early 80s Hasegawa has been choreographing 'natural landscapes' with and within her architecture. She has developed a design sensibility towards light, flexible, scattered and ambiguous realms similar to those experienced in nature. To achieve this, she, like other contemporary Japanese designers including Toyo Ito, Kazunari Sakamoto, Riken Yamamoto, and Kazuyo Sejima, began to extensively employ lightweight industrial materials and products: layered, perforated metallic screens, slim ferrous elements, synthetic fabric, etc. Hasegawa configures these so that while the dispersed and collaged architectural elements are exposed to and animated by light, wind and sound, they also allude to natural formations; they become analogous to some fictive or symbolic landscapes buried in the Japanese collective memory. She says: 'It seems that deep down in their longing, there exists an ideal of Japanese people that has been fostered throughout the long history of an agricultural society. It must be a kind of natural scenery with surrounding mountains, flowing rivers, sweep of rice paddies, lakes and oceans, and scattered houses, shrines, temples. Various architectural symbols of Western and Japanese origin are arranged in typical commercialised houses but my (purpose) is an attempt to trap in natural sceneries . . . by using symbols analogous to nature.'[3]

Hasegawa sets the irreducible qualities of 'nature' and the 'natural' against the increasingly jaded, consumerist urbanscape that seems to besiege nearly every part of the Japanese city today. For her nature is an ally with which to confront the almost total commodification of the whole built environment. She is determined to resist an architecture which is hardly more than a product for consumption, and intends her works as 'poetic machines' that, while capable of 'echoing the call of the past and the distant future', address the conditions of the *present*.[4] Hasegawa's design enterprise therefore is not a 'sentimental journey', a flight from the harsh realities of Japanese urbanism, but a critical venture driving a wedge into those conditions.

The resulting fictive, almost utopian sceneries in

Itsuko Hasegawa, House at Nerima

Riken Yamaoto, Rotunda, Yokohama

Urbanscape in Japan: Tokyo's Shinjuku district

Hiroshi Hara, Yamato International Building, Tokyo

Itsuko Hasegawa, Tokumaru Childrens Clinic, Matsuyama

Kazuo Shinohara, House in Uehara, Tokyo

Hasegawa's designs, however, suggest not only rolling fields, hills and mountains, trees and woods, but also some small vernacular settlements, villages and farming communities that have, by necessity, maintained a close affinity with nature and the natural. Whereas the articulation of an architectural complex as a 'vernacular village' is also apparent in some of the recent designs of other Japanese architects – Hiroshi Hara, Toyo Ito, etc – in Hasegawa's works one can always discover basic elements and/or the filtered image of the prototypical house with its pitched roof, redefined in terms of a 'straightforward' simplicity. The inclusion of a multiplicity of such roofs in the Shonandai Centre is a case in point. In the Shonandai Centre, as well as in many earlier projects: The Bizan Hall (1984), NC Housing (1984), Houses in Nerima (1986), and Kumamoto (1987), she seeks to achieve a merger or at least a certain continuity between natural and built landscapes, between nature and the urban realm and so, also between technology and the elementary, the indigenous. Her return to nature therefore also implies a return to basics and the 'primitive'. In fact, her road toward 'architecture as second nature' began with a strong sympathy for the primitive.

In the 70s, Hasegawa both studied and worked in Kazuo Shinohara's studio at Tokyo Institute of Technology. Her career was thus launched under the influence of her mentor's highly art oriented work. The two shared an interest in an architecture of minimalist/primitive simplicity, yet whereas Shinohara tended toward an abstract, conceptual approach in his efforts to redefine Japanese space, Hasegawa was gradually drawn towards a kind of intuitive or poetic *realism*. Her small residences were arranged in almost direct response to the clients' needs and lifestyles and to the often cramped and irregular sites, rather than being prefigured by some *a priori* conceptual model. Consequently, from the very beginning, Hasegawa's works have been free from the fetish of form or formalism and have had little to do with defining 'architecture as language' either; they have a matter-of-fact quality, revealing the chaotic and paradoxical urban conditions in which they have been invariably conceived and eventually set.

The early works of Hasegawa, quite unlike the previous architecture of the Metabolists in Japan, manifested her loss of interest in the city. Increasingly aware of the rapid and uncontrollably chaotic megalopolitan developments – the growing hazards, congestion, pollution, alienation, etc – she, as many of her contemporaries, was prompted to understand the urban environment as less and less capable of providing a meaningful context for architecture. Therefore her designs, such as the House of Kamoi (1975), House 2 at Yaizu (1977) or House at Midorigaoki (1985), were shaped in defiance of such 'context'; they had the simplest possible form and displayed a most utterly blank expression.

These buildings have all been conceived with a certain objectivity, or as *sächlich* assemblages of formally autonomous parts; yet at the same time, as a 'form' of indifference towards their mediocre environments, the buildings themselves too give the impression of being large fragments of architecture; they appear as sharply focused but only partial 'snapshots' in their proliferating consumerist urbanscape surroundings. In other words, by way of implied primitivism and applied technology, Hasegawa's works of the 1970s provide a manifest contrast to the built landscape; they result from a process of *dissimilation*, and so Hasegawa's architectural realism finds itself clearly at odds with its American counterpart, the contextualism

advocated by Venturi, Stern, Moore and others.

While continuing much of the previous primitivism, dissimilation and critical resistance, Hasegawa's architecture in the early 1980s began to change. The enclosed, inward-oriented designs – her 'disinterested objects' inserted into the 'city of mediocrity' – gradually became more open, clustered, permeable and light, and began to show more interest in the flux and dynamism of urban life. The fragmentary quality of her works has intensified to more actively engage the heterogeneous, collage-like texture of the Japanese city. Simultaneously, the prevailing feeling for the primitive has been complemented by a sense of the natural/vernacular mediated not only by the vestiges of high-tech, but also by a fresh interpretation of technology, that is, the elaboration and use of another kind of technology. Thus, Hasegawa's architecture in the 80s, beyond recollecting images of primal landscapes, old villages and a simple mode of living – along with her newly rediscovered realities in the city – also alludes to a *new technological landscape* and futuristic urban lifestyles.

The first project on the road to a new technology was the House in Kuwahara, Matsuyama in 1980. Here all the various materials and elements – metallic panels and screens, sashes, stainless-steel wire mesh, and other ferrous and non-ferrous components – are used upon the request of the owner, who happened to be a dealer of such materials. The house has thus become, in effect, a sort of showcase of these parts and related technologies, yet without the need or even the possibility to synthesise them into some harmonious whole. Within the simple pitched roofed volumes of the two-storey residence, all constituent parts have a self-claimed independence as they are assembled, or rather collaged, into numerous surfaces, thin structures and screens of different density; the flush-mounted windows have various sizes that disregard the modular network of aluminium panels, steel diagonal braces cross within the openings of the porch and even the sliding glass doors, etc. Technology here has a certain incidental quality.

Both the Bizan Hall, an alumni hall in Shizuoka (1984), and the NC Housing with 12 bachelor apartments in Tokyo (1984) are larger complexes with a more extensive application of industrially produced components and technology. If the House in Kuwahara is shaped by the circumstances of the available materials used, these two multi-storey buildings have been configured, almost literally, by the need to utilise their extremely tight and irregular sites to the maximum allowable limits. Other confines have been height limit and provisions of insulation. Not only complying with, but in fact taking advantage of these unfavourable conditions in a stoic manner, Hasegawa's designs are put together cumulatively from numerous spatial, formal and structural parts, some of which are repetitive, like the pyramidal roofs and skylights, others are mutually unrelated; these latter would include, in both cases, the vaulted roof elements for example.

In the selection of materials, again industrially produced and readily available, ordinary ones dominate. Their use is particularly relevant when they highlight specific technological/structural solutions. The steel tension cable structure of the canopy over the entrance way to the Bizan Hall, for example, recalls works and projects by the Russian Constructivists as well as Norman Foster and Richard Rogers. This is, however, with a slightly distorted angle along the converging lines of a triangle which, with the outcome of site conditions, imparts the experience of accelerated perspective.

The analogy of Constructivism here is all the more appropriate since, like its representatives in the early 1920s, Hasegawa intends to eliminate the distinctions between architecture, technology and everyday life, while criticising the snobbish aspirations of high-art. Indeed, the Constructivist slogan: 'Down with Art! Long live technology!... Long live the Constructivist Technician!' seems to approximate, implicitly at least, Hasegawa's recent intentions.[5]

Within these works so far, it is important to recognise Hasegawa's shift of emphasis in design. In the case of the House in Kuwahara, technology was mobilised in order to recollect the prototypical house with its 'primitive' vernacular; in the latter two cases the spectrum of technology's role has been broadened to also envision clusters of vernacular shelters, or indigenous villages and, perhaps, also rolling hills and mountains – what Hasegawa refers to in describing both the Bizan Hall and the House in Kumamoto of 1986.[6] Two consecutive residences provide additional departures towards evoking nature by technological details; the Houses in Nerima (1986) and Oyamadai (1988), as much as some earlier, unrealised projects, beyond the already mentioned elements, both employ aluminium screens that are patterned with undulating edges, as 'explicit' reminders of such natural formations as hills, waves, clouds, tree foliage, etc.

The House in Nerima reinforces this by its softly curving roofs covered by corrugated, metallic sheets, over a complex of terraces and an additional 'moon-viewing' deck. A combination of both reinforced concrete and slim steel frame structures, the house is remarkably airy, permeable, and, with ample open air spaces under the floating roofs, it is penetrated by nature – wind, light, etc – in a manner that is rather similar to that of Toyo Ito's recent designs with lightweight structures, represented particularly well by his own residence, the Silver Hut in Tokyo (1984). In both these houses by Hasegawa, just like in the case of Ito's design, intricately articulated courtyards help break up the solidity of architectural volumes to suggest the domestic realm by layering all the elements, screens of various density, the lightweight steel stairways, and many others in a straightforward yet intuitive manner. Undoubtedly, technology is approached and utilised here not with an overwhelming and rigid rationality, but rather by way of what may be called 'fuzzy logic', and a unique sensibility that, endowing these works, activate the 'poetic machines' of Hasegawa.

In the Shonandai Centre and the Interior Pavilion for the Nagoya World Design Exposition (1989), this process, that is the combination of nature and technology, has been further accelerated. Both projects include extensive outdoor areas which are designed with the overwhelming application of thin, semi-transparent metallic screens, various tree-like devices of aluminium and/or fibreglass reinforced plastic and, in the Shonandai, also of the glittering spheres of a world globe, a cosmic globe, a moon globe and a geodesic dome; whereas at the Pavilion, of milky-white tent structures of synthetic Quilin. All this sophisticated, 'technological' apparatus with a material substance reduced to supple surfaces, is mobilised here to 'reflect the sky and change colours like clouds or the sea, blurring the buildings' outline', and in so doing, to 'suggest an entirely new kind of nature', as Hasegawa herself wrote.[7] Moreover both these projects also suggest a kind of high-tech camping, or a travelling circus, that is to say, something temporary and hence suitable for Japan's new 'urban nomads'.[8] Yet these

qualities, as Hajime Yatsuka observed, can also evoke scenes as naive as a 'fairy-tale village on the moon out of a children's book'.[9]

The shift in focus in Hasegawa's designs with regard to technology represents a growing trend in Japanese architecture which has to be understood first, against the Modernist interpretation of technology, then later on, against the so called High-Tech architecture and further, more specifically, in relation to the Japanese preoccupation with technology in general, best exemplified by the Metabolist movement in the 1960s. Modern architecture was born as a result of the technological revolution taking place in the early 20th century wherein technology was regarded as universal. Consequently, Modernism was carried on towards standardisation and eventually the anonymity of design. In the mechanical world of the first machine age, despite the increasingly sophisticated modes of manufacturing, with mass production, prefabrication, module-coordination and rational systematisation as dominant forces, the strong tendency towards universalisation in architecture intensified. An unwavering faith of the modernists in the powers of technological progress led to approaching even urban design and urbanism by way of technology.

Metabolism, the last representative of Modern architecture in Japan, projected the vision of a technological landscape which was as much megastructural as it was all-encompassing. Technology, endowed with a powerful mythical quality, was believed to be capable of correcting all the fallacies of both the physical environment or the city, and society itself, by casting a systematic order over the urban disorder. Kenzo Tange's Tokyo Plan, 1960, along with other visionary and utopian projects by Kikutake, Kurokawa, and even Isozaki to some extent, envisioned, if not always by explicit intention then certainly as a consequence, a unified urbanscape and a controllable, well operating urban machine that was fuelled and run by industrial technology. The Modernist/Metabolist landscape and the city were derivative of a technology of *hardware* that was, in principle and sometimes quite literally, imposed from above. The idealised mechanism of such a 'machine' and technology could only work over and above the given reality of the existing city.

Then in 1970, with the closing of the Osaka Expo-70, the grandiose showcase of a universal technological progress in Japan, and with the eventual demise of Metabolist ideology, the modernist and anonymous technological landscape as an operative model for the future collapsed. The events of the 1970s – energy crisis, economic recession, the revelation of the 'dark side' of progress, etc – necessarily instigated first the rejection, then the re-evaluation of technology. The meaning of technology had to change, and has changed significantly since the early 1980s, even if universal Modernism, disguised in sleek, high-tech architectural packages, seems to persevere.

What are the general symptoms of this change? First of all, architects began to descend from the 'clouds and sky' and, with an attitude closer to actual reality and more down to earth, were prompted to look at the city through the eyes of its ordinary citizens. Such new positions, while they could not afford the view of the whole but only fragmentary vistas, provided the conditions of immediate and direct yet partial interventions which, although not ideal solutions, seemed to work. Technology has lost its claim to universality and has become more locally inflected and realistic. Therefore, the new technological landscape is analogous to the multi-layered Japanese urbanscape; it operates in

Arata Isozaki, Joint Core System, project from the city in the Sky series

Kenzo Tange, Osaka Expo-70 Spaceframe over the festival Plaza

Kazuo Shinohara, TIT Centennial Hall, Tokyo

Fumihiko Maki, Spiral Building, Tokyo

Shin Takamatsu, Kirin Plaza Building, Osaka

Shin Takamatsu, Week Building, Kyoto

and produces heterogeneities rather than striving for homogeneity. In other words, the new technology in architecture is now capable of addressing contradictory conditions; and often, even its own operation is paradoxical, it results in an architecture of and by 'autonomous' parts, and further, a 'fragmented landscape'.

The 'architectural machine' and the landscape this technology produces is thus non-structural, or more precisely, post-structuralist and, as such, non-hierarchical. Rather, the new technological landscape is network-like and so, more akin to a computer *software* whose overall order is hidden or undecipherable but, like a programme conceived along a 'fuzzy logic', is more episodic and flexible, and whose 'organisation' represents what the French philosopher Gilles Deleuze termed *corps sans organes* (body without organs).[11] In other words, it is a curious patchwork which, while not providing a radical alternative to the existing urbanscape, in the best cases manages to change it into an altogether different one.[12]

Today there is a plethora of architects who turn to a new 'soft' technology in order to respond to, and often critically address, the paradoxical and unprecedentedly fast-changing built environment which, indeed, either as a fast running 'computer programme' or as a new 'second nature', acquires an ambiguous, but more *ephemeral* quality. Other designers who reinterpret technology in a new but *personal* way in addition to Hasegawa, include Shinohara, Maki, Hara, Ito, Sakamoto, Yamamoto, Sejima, Hajime Yatsuka and Shin Takamatsu. Their works display as much disparity as similarity in this respect. In their architecture, while tectonic considerations continue to play an important role in most cases, they do not claim overall primacy. On the one hand, unlike the heavy megastructural schemes of the Metabolists, the physical and tectonic entity of many new structures tends to acquire a certain lightness, often approximating an 'immaterial evocation of building'. Yet, in so doing, the actual but 'simple' mode of fabrication is still (or again) a significant aspect. This line of design often addresses the issue of construction in such a straightforward or *sächlich* manner that only vernacular and primitive architecture could do before. Ito, talking about his Silver Hut, described the quality of this design: 'A primitive hut designed for dwelling in a modern, urban environment, just as ancient people made their primitive huts with logs, would be (a) silver coloured hut as is this house, made of metallic materials which are easily available today.'[13] Among Hasegawa's works it is perhaps the House in Nerima which best represents such 'primitive' construction.

On the other hand, we find another kind of architecture that aspires to technology, but wherein tectonics is in effect either insignificant in articulating architecture and/or is covered up by scenography. Yet, in this case, interestingly enough, what actually covers architecture is an imitation of technology. As in Shin Takamatsu's architecture of 'dead-tech', technology is rendered merely as a system of signs sometimes both metaphorically and figuratively. To exemplify this, the Kirin Plaza in Osaka (1988) should be pointed out. Here, technology is both an appliqué on the facade and a computer controlled system of electric signs, whose flickering lights are meant to continue the electrographic nightscape of the city.

Needless to say, most works that constitute the new technological landscape fall between the two polarities: a nature and environment-sensitive 'industrial vernacular' architecture either with a 'primitive' or sophisticated 'software' technology, and a highly scenographic, theatrical architecture, often with 'only' a simulated technology. The first is activated and 'shaped' by various natural phenomena and/or the flux of city life, and thus, displays a tendency toward formal and spatial impermanence; the other is propelled by the imperatives of image making, and tends to be highly formal or formalistic and often monumental in its appearance.

To illustrate, two examples come to mind: Ito's Tower of Wind (1986) is a multi-layered semi-permeable cylindrical device that wraps around a huge ventilation outlet of the underground shopping plaza in front of Yokohama Station. Within its thin, punched aluminium and acrylic layers, 4,000 evenly distributed electric bulbs light up according to a computer programme that is fed through sensors monitoring and then displaying, in continuously altering and unpredictable patterns, the changing direction and velocity of wind, intensity of noise or sound, degree of temperature, etc, in the night: a poetic machine indeed. Yet, just as Ito has his tower of wind, so does Hasegawa: the Shonandai Centre also includes a 'tower of wind and light' similarly 'activated by light, wind and sound'.[14]

The second example is another Takamatsu work, the Week Building in Kyoto (1986) which displays 'dismembered' elements of a huge 'machine' as they scatter across the facade of the building. Yet, this technology-as-appliqué or sign is not unknown in Hasegawa's architecture either. Her Atelier in Tomigaya (1987) features a long, diagonal steel space frame and steel cables that allude to the image of a crane. Obviously, this 'technology' has not much to do with the particular way the building is built; as it divorces itself from technique or the art of making, and from actual use, the 'crane' approximates the quality of what Kenneth Frampton has termed pure or '*instrumental* sign'.[15] And, as such, this technology also borders on the threshold of populism (can this be pop-tech?) and perhaps even entertainment. Ultimately, like many representatives of New-Tech in Japanese architecture, including Osamu Ishiyama's early seminal work, the Fantasy Villa in Omi of 1975, neither the Shonandai nor the Nagoya Fair Pavilion is completely devoid of such qualities.[16]

In this sense, Hasegawa's latest projects reveal new aspects that both broaden the horizon of her design possibilities and increase the risks involved. The combination of contemporary technology with a 'primitive' simplicity, in addition to producing a new industrial vernacular and yielding a cosmic dimension (note again the large spherical elements or globes) in the Shonandai Centre, now also bears a certain affinity with the simulated world of Disney. The future success of Hasegawa's 'architecture as second nature' presented by way of her new interpretation of technology, will ultimately depend upon whether she is able to avoid succumbing to, while flirting with or utilising, the tempting world of simulations in order to shift the course of recent, consumerist urban development towards new realities. Hasegawa's work is certainly worth watching in the l990s.

Notes

1 Itsuko Hasegawa, '3 Projects', *The Japan Architect*, Nov/Dec, 1986, p 55.

2 I Hasegawa, 'Architecture as Second Nature', *The Japan Architect,* Nov/Dec, 1989, p 17.

3 I Hasegawa, 'Natural Scenery, Analogy of Nature' in *Itsuko Hasegawa*, special issue of *Space Design*, Tokyo, April, 1985, p 17.

4 I Hasegawa, 'Urbanism and the Poetic Machine', *ibid*, p 55.

5 Quoted by Kenneth Frampton 'Constructivism' in V M Lampugnani, *Encyclopedia of 20th-Century Architecture*, H N Abrams, New York 1986, p 71.

6 I Hasegawa *op cit*, note 3.

7 I Hasegawa, 'Interior Pavilion of the World Design Exposition', *The Japan Architect,* Nov/Dec, 1989, p 24.

8 Toyo Ito in reference to his recent architecture borrows the term 'urban nomads' from the French philosophers Gilles Deleuze and Félix Guattari, T Ito, 'Project for the Restaurant NOMAD, 1986', *Space Design*, Sept, 1986, p 32.

9 Hajime Yatsuka, 'An Architecture Floating on the Sea of Signs', in B Bognar ed *Japanese Architecture*, special issue of *Architectural Design* , Vol 58 No 5/6, 1988, p 10.

10 Botond Bognar, 'Archaeology of a Fragmented Landscape' in B Bognar ed *Japanese Architecture, op cit*, note 9, p 15.

11 Gilles Deleuze and Felix Guattari, *Mille Plateaux*, Editions de Minuit, Paris, 1980. Also published as *A Thousand Plateaus – Capitalism and Schizophrenia*, translation and foreword by Brian Massumi, University of Minnesota Press, Minneapolis, 1987.

12 H Yatsuka, 'The Technological Landscape' in *Itsuko Hasegawa, op cit*, note 3, p 68.

13 Toyo Ito, 'Primitive Hut in the Modern City', *The Japan Architect*, May, 1985, p 30.

14 I Hasegawa, *op cit*, note 2.

15 K Frampton, 'Towards a Critical Regionalism: Six Points for an Architecture of Resistance', in Hal Foster ed, *The Anti- Aesthetic*, Bay Press, Port Townsend, WA, 1983, p 21.

16 With regard to an early application of a new technology, Osamu Ishiyama's Fantasy Villa in Omi (Aichi Prefecture) of 1975 has to be acknowledged. In this project, as the best representative of his 'sewer pipe' or 'junk' architecture, Ishiyama assembled, in an *ad-hoc* fashion, a small weekend house from readily available industrial components, ferrous products and by-products not necessarily meant for architecture. The result is as much a unique 'industrial', primitive hut as it is a 'fairy tale' house for children. The Villa therefore also exemplifies well the combination of the two kinds of new technology: a primitive and a popular one.

Botond Bognar is professor of architecture at the University of Illinois, Urbana-Champaign, and author of several books on Japanese architecture.

STANLEY TIGERMAN
OTHER ARCHITECTURAL PROBLEMS
and Recent Projects

The abstraction that increasingly mutes our understanding of architecture as a series of readable forms has developed out of the architect's insistence that certain problems inherent in the discipline necessarily create ambiguity. These dissident elements blur the clarity conventionally inscribed on the facade of the House of Architecture. While many issues faced by architects can be considered in this light, four are of particular interest: *Stasis*: a state in which opposite forces of equal strength serve to cancel each other out; *Mimesis*: an imitation or representation; *Otherness*: a reliance on things extrinsic to architecture for definition, rather than an examination of intrinsic qualities; and *Synthesis*: the assembling of separate or subordinate forms into a whole, ie, a new form. These problems, in particular, arise from our perception that architecture is an expression of something other than itself. Taken separately, these dissident elements may help illuminate the discipline known as 'the mother of the arts', which has become increasingly opaque even as contemporary practitioners employ a variety of means to resolve what they perceive to be essential ambiguities.

Stasis: The myth that architecture is static is continually reinforced by our perception that buildings do not move. Of course, we know that gravity slowly and almost imperceptibly causes bodies, as well as buildings, to compress. It is impossible to resist those forces that pull us back to the soil from which, according to the Bible, we arose. What is not immediately apparent about stasis is the enormous energy required to maintain this resistance. The constituent elements of architecture – columns, beams, trusses, girders, walls – have a natural propensity to separate from one another, to become dynamic. The conventional ways in which these elements are assembled in construction dramatically defy such natural forces as gravity and lateral movement. Only the most extraordinary measures prevent the whole from disintegrating into discrete parts. A conventional force diagram shows structural elements contending with gravity, creating the appearance of stasis; their very name, 'compression members', indicates the direction in which they will ultimately, albeit slowly, move.

The theory that opposing forces create equilibrium speaks to the interdependency of architectural elements on many levels. In certain circumstances, projects evolve specifically from the notion that stasis can be internalised; that opposing forces can be given clear and direct expression in both form and programme. In the Instant City Project of 1965-66, for example, angled planes create semi-pyramidal volumes that house entire cities, and exterior grids reflect the internal structural geometry. 'Countervalence' also describes the balance of opposing forces, an equilibrium in which the potential for deterioration is implicit in the particularities of juxtaposition.

Architecture is always in the process of being destabilised,

even as it appears to resist this action by its very nature. While it is possible to understand that a building, like a baby, begins to die at birth, this course is not easily accepted in the consideration of architecture, a discipline continually revalidated by historicism.

The inference of disintegration in an interdependent relationship is particularly explicit in the work of sculptor Kenneth Snelson. Every element of the composition is dependent on every other element, such that the displacement of one causes the collapse of the whole. The vulnerability of the construction is clear. Bridges of the bascule type are structures in the process of transformation even as we perceive them to be in an equivalent state.

An immense amount of energy is required to convey the impression of stasis. While we may perceive stability, deterioration is the implicit kinetic subtext. The collapse of apparently static essences, in which they flow, change velocity, and ultimately change in appearance, is a powerful force with which the architect must contend. Stasis challenges the architect to develop forms that actualise compositions of counterpoised physical elements. Such architecture subverts precedent, and thus can be seen as rising outside the parameters described and given authority by the discipline's historical evolution. Nonetheless, each generation of architects is obligated to confront stasis afresh; witness the 1988 'Deconstructivist Architecture' exhibition at the MoMA in New York. In this exhibition, however, art history was employed to exploit the precedent of Russian Constructivism. This methodology served to neutralise the work of a generation of architects determined to deflect architecture from a trajectory informed by the use of historical antecedents for validation.

Otherness: From generation to generation, it seems as though architects have been determined to define their craft through the examination of issues extrinsic to architecture. They seek definition in the consideration of function, structure and stylistic referentiality rather than looking within architecture's own precinct to discover what, if anything, constitutes its essence. Among the many extrinsic operations that seduce architects away from investigating from within, metaphor and metonymy are among the most often employed.

Metaphor, in which one object is likened to another by referring to it as if it were that other, has been a technique favoured throughout the history of Western architecture. The Brown Derby restaurant in Los Angeles is a parody which exemplifies the problems of metaphoric referentiality in architecture. The metaphor has *become* the form, and thus has a hollow ring.

Metonymy, in which, linguistically, a thing is named by one of its attributes, is another operation common in the practice of architecture, where a thing is made to resemble one of its attributes. Again, forms do not express their own

Park Lane Hotel, Kyoto, 1990, model view

Sculpture by Kenneth Snelson

Bascule-bridge

The Brown Derby, Los Angeles

Stanley Tigerman,
Formica Showroom,
Chicago, 1986

Skidmore, Owings &
Merrill, Tigerman
McCurry, Frank Gehry,
et al, King's Cross
project, London, 1988

Michael Markham, study
of Chicago Federal
Center Complex, 1988

essence; rather they stand in for the displaced original. The various iterations of the several temples of the Jews, with the Temple of Solomon as the original precedent, are examples of metonymic operations not wholly determined by mimesis. A metonymic Christian equivalent of the temple speculations can be found in the several Renaissance designs for St Peter's in Rome.

Beyond metaphor and metonymy, functionalism, formalism, structural expressionism and regionalism are among the many approaches available to divert the architect from an examination of the intrinsic qualities of his discipline. This need for, and accessibility of, an 'other', a meaning or a process that can be externally imposed, perpetually defers the architect's potential to probe and ultimately illuminate his craft from within – a far more challenging process.

In order to resist such distracting and pervasive temptations, it is necessary to conceive of an architecture stripped of the myriad conventions that have traditionally defined and refined it. In one example of such an exploration, a 1984 tableau for a niche at the Deutsches Architekturmuseum in Frankfurt aims to describe man's original, albeit mythical, home. The space is conceptually measured in a three-dimensional grid of cubits. The gridded Garden of Eden attempts unsuccessfully to contain two trees standing for Adam and Eve, the branches of which interrupt the module as they grow up and out. In the Formica Showroom installed at Chicago's Merchandise Mart in 1986, the design is meant to suggest the presence of the product while positing the absence of the architecture that presumably brought it into being; the product does not require extrinsic elements to verify or even justify its existence. The gridded showroom space suggests scaffolding, implying something in the process of becoming, or, conversely, of being removed. These exploratory gestures seek to strip away inherited conventions that distract from the contemplation of *dwelling* and *being*, architecture's etymological origins. They resist subjection to the condition of being 'secondary', or extrinsic, rather than 'primary', or intrinsic. Plato's charge that 'art is in the shadow of truth' is perpetuated in architecture when practitioners distance themselves from the essence of their craft by engaging in acts of 'otherness'.

Mimesis: In architecture (or anything else) mimesis arises from disillusionment with the present. This disillusionment is spawned by an exaggerated belief in the power of precedent to validate contemporary design, particularly through reiteration. Relied upon particularly in epochs when collective insecurity prevails, mimesis and the condition that brought it about are clearly apparent in the Renaissance, for example. Chaucer, Spenser and Shakespeare are among the many writers that defined this malaise from a literary vantage point, as A Bartlett Giammati points out in *Exile and Change in Renaissance Literature*, but it is the artists and architects of the period who most poignantly expressed the permeating sense of loss. By first removing the divine being from the 'centre' so ecclesiastic architecture predating that period (beginning with the two trees in the centre of the garden of Eden and ending with the Gothic cathedral in the centre of the square), and then positioning man in what was originally a space occupied only by a divine being, the architects of the Renaissance reinforced feelings of collective insecurity about the perpetuation of siting God in a place that they wished to inhabit; notwithstanding the popular belief that the Renaissance was a time that captured all of history for its own purposes.

By mimetically reiterating forms and processes that derive from Greco-Roman precedents, Renaissance architects attempted to validate their own epoch. It is possible to read their achievement as, inadvertently, having the opposite effect: if detached from the corroboration of history, their work would be insufficient to provide new sources of inspiration. Succumbing to overwhelming nostalgic desires to intersect with a divine being by replacing it, the architects of the day engaged in reiterative projects in order to substantiate their belief that they were the logical inheritors of the past.

Georgian London is an example of a second-generation attempt to explain the power of both the original, in this case the architecture of Ancient Greece and Rome, and the first-generation antecedent, the architecture of the Renaissance. The authority of contextualism is overwhelming. In attempts to elaborate on it, architects inevitably surrender to precedent and often go so far as to mimic it, creating the impression that nothing new has transpired since the origination of the form. The 1988 King's Cross project in London, collaborated on by Skidmore, Owings & Merrill, Tigerman McCurry, Frank O Gehry, and others, is a good example of this practice.

Repetition begets sycophancy, as Palladio begot Scamozzi (Teatro Olimpico, Vicenza) and Mies van der Rohe begot numerous descendants (such as Lake Shore Drive). The Miesian acolytes, in particular, represent a generation of architects committed to mimesis. Without expanding on the language evolved by Mies, his descendants mimetically reproduce contrived iterations of the original.

The problem with mimesis is that once a commitment is made to a position of perpetual imperfection, the probability of ever again engaging in original thought is reduced to an imperceptible minimum. Locked into a position that will always be removed from the original, the mime is guaranteed the rewards of imperfection, the flaws and defects connected with playing that role. Resisting that position, and indeed searching for an alternative, becomes the obligation of individuals in each successive generation of architects who accept the responsibility of giving representation to an optimistic belief in renewal.

The 1989 design for the Fukuoka City apartment complex in Kiushu, Japan, is informed by a concentration on measurement, through the use of a grid, which is intended to deflect the semantic trajectory informing much of contemporary architecture. Even as this project attempts to resist the mimetic tendencies of architectural production, however, it is nostalgically inclined towards reconstruction and the recovery of the inaccessible garden of Eden, represented by the building's enclosed courtyard.

Synthesis: The final problem is that presented by synthesis, in which separate or subordinate parts are assembled into a whole. The tradition of architecture is, in part, based on a determined search for closure. Closure, in architectural terms, is the amalgamation of disparate forces into new forms. Synthesis comes about through the subordination of constituent parts to an essence that is determined to be the whole, ie, more than the sum of such parts. Seldom does a building have equivalent representation of all elements that have gone into its formulation.

The problem of privileging one element over another in the quest for closure is endemic to the synthetic process. It is as if antithesis evolves only as a 'straw man' to be overturned so as to perpetuate the original thesis as a way of rationalising it. In architectural terms deterioration is implicit in pre-Modernist, or closed, forms, as assuredly as closure is implied by Post-Modernist forms.

University of Illinois at Chicago graduate architecture student Michael Markham's 1988 project, shows that the potential for deterioration exists in Mies van der Rohe's Chicago Federal Center complex, which is conventionally perceived as a series of closed forms. Markham's study reveals that Mies' compositional organisation has within it the possibility of its own deconstruction; witness the 'open' corner in Mies's buildings as vestiges of earlier, compositionally 'open', forms. The converse is true in the plan of Sir Edwin Lutyens' Gray Walls project in Scotland, as well as in Frank Lloyd Wright's 1908 Robie House plan. While in both of the latter examples the architects began to fragment the classical or traditional plan, the 'closed' forms on which they are based are clearly present.

Dialectical theories are seldom so equivalent in their positioning that stability, or the equilibrium of opposing elements, is achieved or can be sustained. The difficulty of producing an architecture that does not privilege one element over another remains one of the greatest challenges an architect faces.

The practice of unresolved dialectics is one strategy available to architects who feel determined to resist the pressure of synthesis. The problem with this strategy is that it goes against the humanism, the optimistic spirit that has always imbued architectural production. This approach has value in the short term, however, as it opens up possibilities not always available through the use of synthesis.

(In)Conclusive Conclusion: The study of these problems has occupied me, and manifests itself in my architectural production, in recent years. These studies have grown out of an increasing dissatisfaction with architecture as a secondary, rather than a primary, pursuit; ie, the avoidance of the study of architecture innately. While I have no conclusive proof that architecture has constituent features that could identify it as being primary, my suspicions are that this is the case. Secretly, I think that measurement is the constituent feature of architecture. The burden of history weighing down a discipline such as architecture, with the continuous need for (re)validation, is perpetually enervating. It is necessary to identify problems that delimit this human activity so as to reconstitute it in a primary, as well as a secondary, way, as it is generally acknowledged that architecture is multivalent.

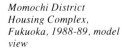
Momochi District Housing Complex, Fukuoka, 1988-89, model view

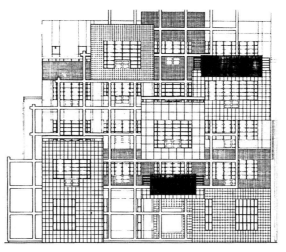

MOMOCHI DISTRICT HOUSING COMPLEX, FUKUOKA

This complex was built as one of two American exhibits in the housing component of the 1989 Asian-Pacific Exposition in Japan. It is built on reclaimed land on a waterfront site, and will remain as the seed for future development of a residential neighbourhood.

This six-storey structure is comprised of retail spaces located on the ground floor and condominium units on the remaining five floors. The structure is responsive to the shifting angles of the sun, so crucial to housing developments in Japan, and proportioned by use of the Japanese system of the ken.

The lobby provides the only access to a square, central garden, the perimeters of which are bounded by the building while open to the sky. The condominium units are reached by circumnavigating this central space, and all open to the street by at least one exterior balcony. The interior garden is marked by a clean, unbroken white grid, while the black grid of the exterior elevation is used to reassemble the disparate elements of the building as an act of reconstruction. Marked by grey ceramic tiles of different sizes, the apartments vary in their individual responses to functional concerns.

OPPOSITE PAGE: Window detail and lobby
ABOVE, LEFT AND BELOW: View of courtyard, west elevation, interior view (of exhibition opening), exterior view and north elevation

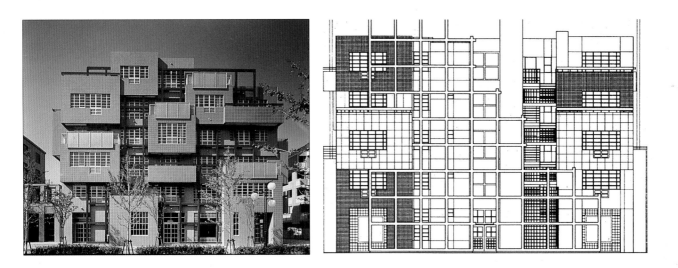

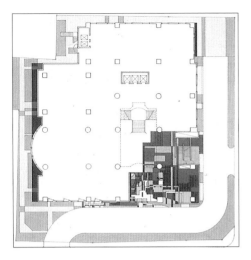

PARK LANE HOTEL, KYOTO

The Programme: Tigerman McCurry was asked to design the facade of a new 14-storey 220 room hotel located in Kyoto. The floor plans and the shape of the building were provided by Daiken Architects and Engineering in Tokyo.

The Design Concept: The building volume was an 'el' shape in the x, y, and z axis. Thanks to the exploration work of Eisenman, we know that this is a topological 'el'. The significance here is that a topological 'el' is based upon a proportional relationship to all of its sides. Because of this relationship, what affects one axis (the x, for example) has the potential to affect the other two axes (the y and z).

Two primary streets define the south and

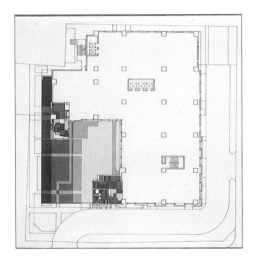

west edges of the block occupied by this buiding, while the north and east edges are defined by secondary streets. This block (the 'site') occupies the south-west corner of a superblock. This superblock (the 'context') is defined by the same primary streets as the site to the south and west, while the north and east are bound by two additional primary streets. It becomes clear that the site and context, along with the building, are defined by an 'el' in plan.

The Strategy: The similarities in plan of the building, the site and the context, along with the proportional relationships that were previously established within the building, led to the development of the facades. The first step was to establish a system that allowed the

interplay of the building, the site and the context. The property line, at the scale with respect to the building, was used as a registration devise. The site was scaled to fit within the property line of the building and superposed with the building. Similarly, the context was scaled to fit within the property line of the building and superposed with both the building and the site information. The second step was to continue this within the boundary of the existing property line setting up a recursive relationship between the building, the site and the context. The result of these moves are, in effect, three buildings, sites and contexts at three different scales, defining one project. This process was carefully recorded with the aid of

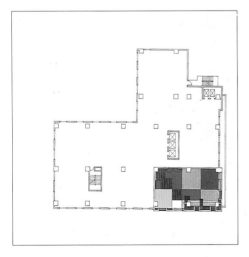

colour as a coding device to help map the density of each superposition. The third step was to take advantage of the proportional relationships that were established and translate the topology of the project in plan to elevation. At four locations (Entry, Tea Ceremony Room, Health Club, and Governor's Suite) the texture becomes embedded within the original topological 'el' and affects the interior space. The 'el' however, is the least articulated allowing the difference of the original shape to be shown.

OPPOSITE PAGE: Model view
ABOVE, LEFT AND BELOW: Ground floor plan, north elevation, third floor plan, 12th and 13th floor plan and east elevation

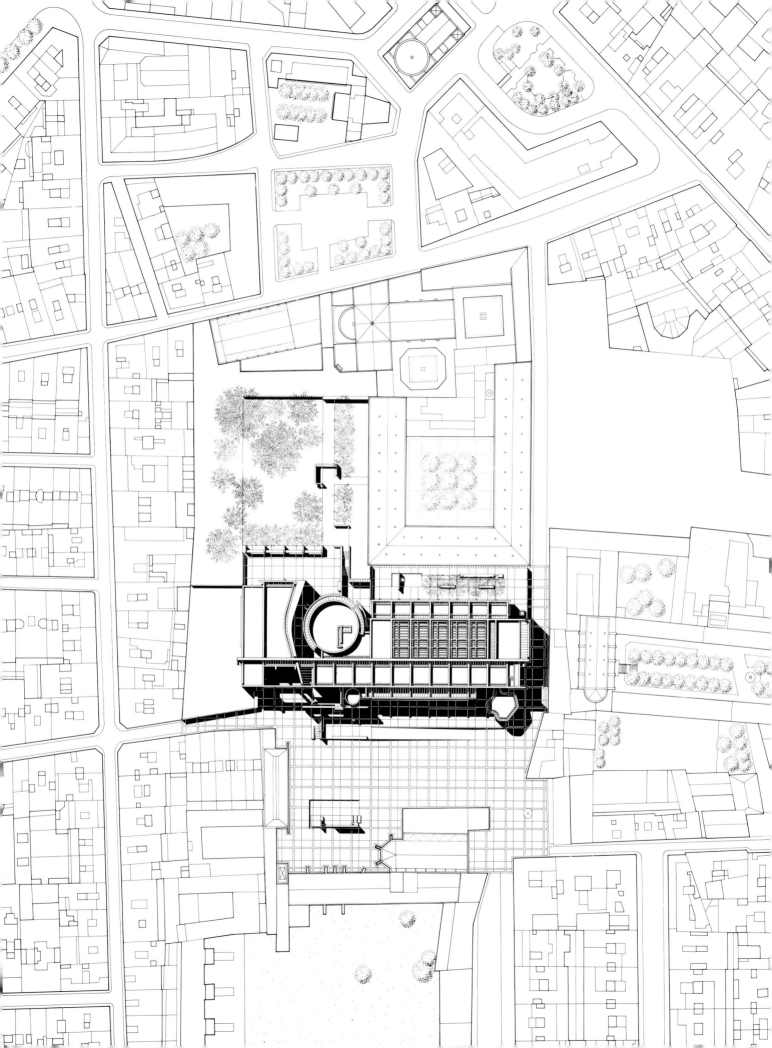

RICHARD MEIER

MUSEUM OF CONTEMPORARY ART, BARCELONA

Located in the area of the Casa de la Caritat, previously a monastic enclave, the Museum of Contemporary Art in Barcelona creates a dialogue between the historic forms of its outer context and the contemporary art within. The labyrinthian nature of the surrounding urban fabric is reflected in the fundamental organisation of the building. This is perhaps most evident in the main entrance which runs parallel to the passage allowing free pedestrian movement between the museum garden to the rear of the block, and a newly created pedestrian plaza and urban core to be known as the Plaça dels Angels. (This paseo will form part of an existing pedestrian network running throughout the old city like a cultural promenade, connecting various civic institutions). Access to the ground floor entry, raised one metre above the general level of the plaza, is afforded by a generously dimensioned ramp.

Having passed through the principal portico, visitors enter into a cylindrical reception area that affords a clear view over the interpenetrating paseo. From this initial reception space the circulation continues along an interior ramp, located within a ramped hall of treble height that gives views of the galleries as well as the plaza. In addition to serving as an orientation device, this louvred hall helps to filtre any natural light entering the museum from the south. The principal gallery

spaces are situated close to the entry drum. They parallel, in their bulk and placement, the general mass of the Casa de la Caritat located behind the museum. These exhibition volumes comprise large, open, loft-like spaces that can easily accommodate sizeable contemporary works.

Possibly the most striking feature of this exhibition sequence is the layering of space from the louvred ramp hall, on the plaza, through to the double-height gallery which runs the full length of the north-eastern facade. Visitors must cross over full-height light 'slots', complete with glass-lensed floors, to enter the main galleries or to pass from these to the viewing balconies overlooking the double-height space to the north-east.

This overall exhibition sequence is complemented by a series of irregularly shaped galleries, stacked in the south-western wing behind the paseo wall. These are intended for the exhibition of small-scale works such as prints, photographs and drawings. Beyond these galleries, to the extreme south-west of the block, lies the administrative wing comprising a research library, an education centre, a museum shop and a small cafe.

While keeping a low profile and harmonising within its urban context, the light-patterns of this museum will patently bestow upon a medieval core a totally new rhythm of movement and energy.

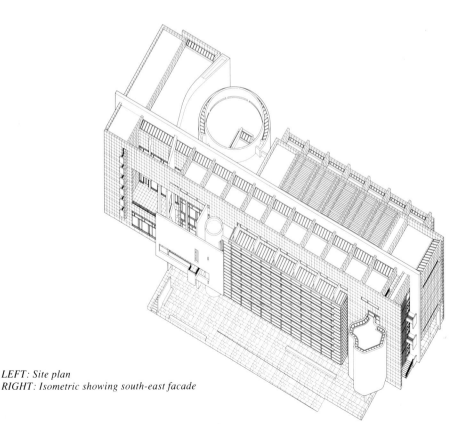

LEFT: Site plan
RIGHT: Isometric showing south-east facade

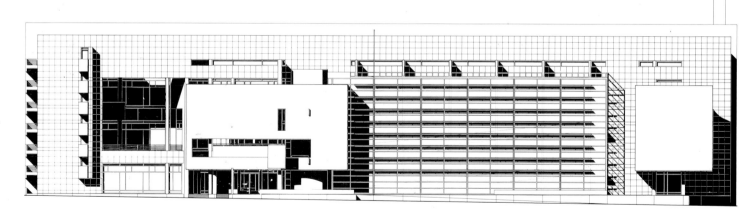

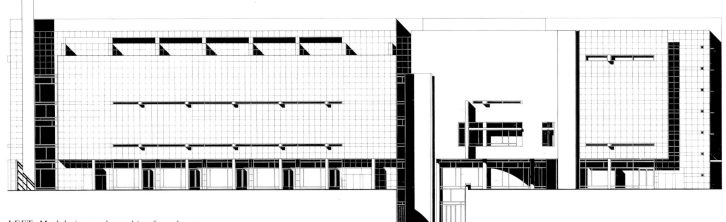

LEFT: *Model view and graphic of south-east elevation*
ABOVE: *Model view of south-east elevation and graphic of north-west elevation*

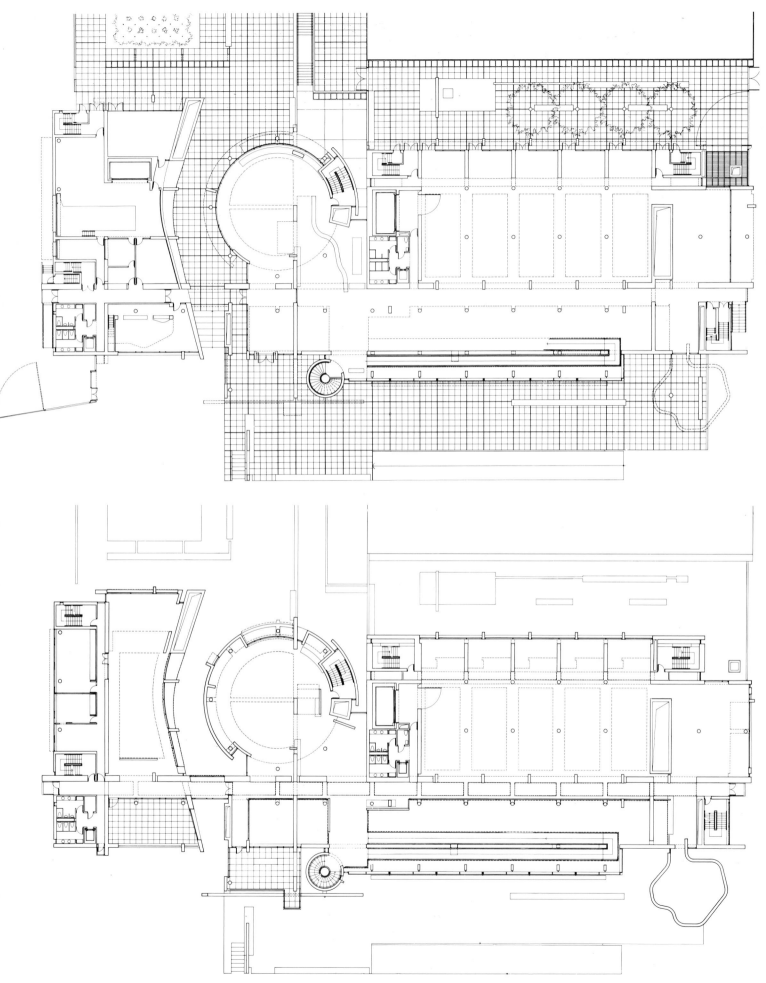

50

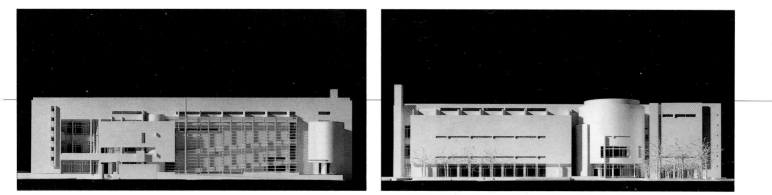

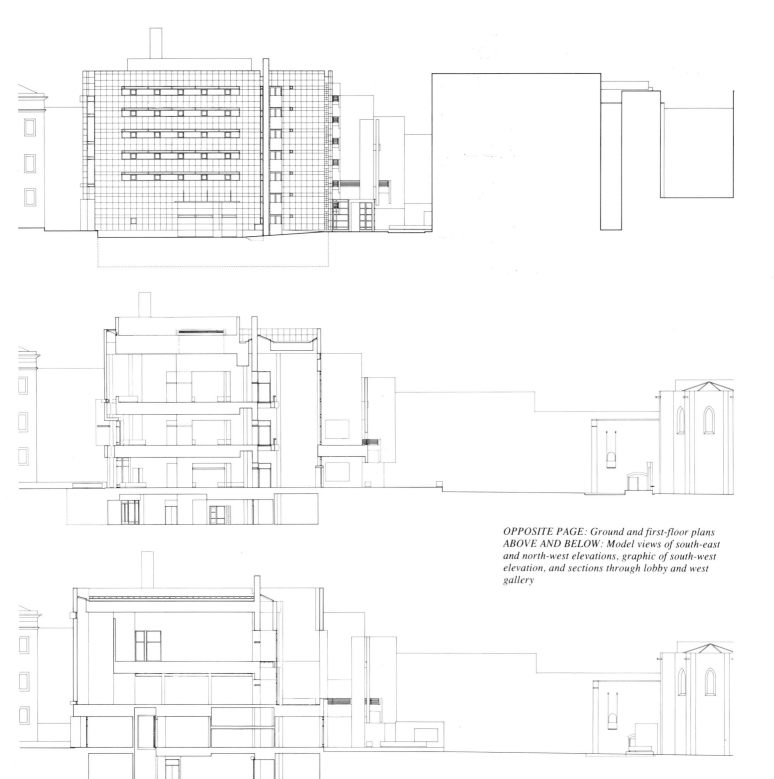

*OPPOSITE PAGE: Ground and first-floor plans
ABOVE AND BELOW: Model views of south-east
and north-west elevations, graphic of south-west
elevation, and sections through lobby and west
gallery*

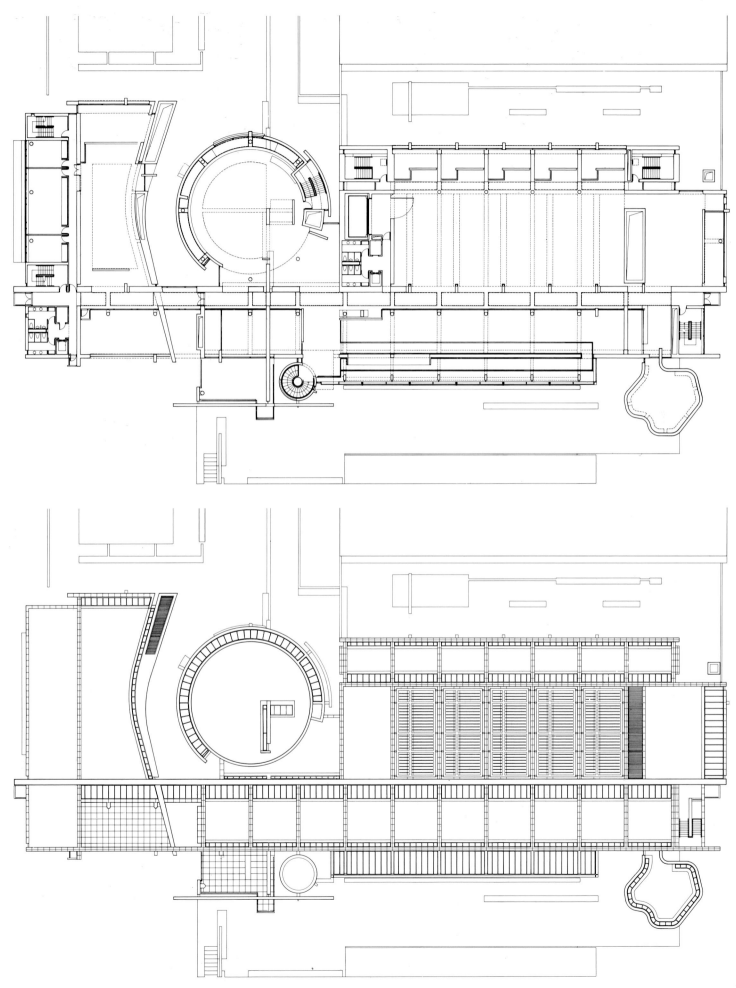

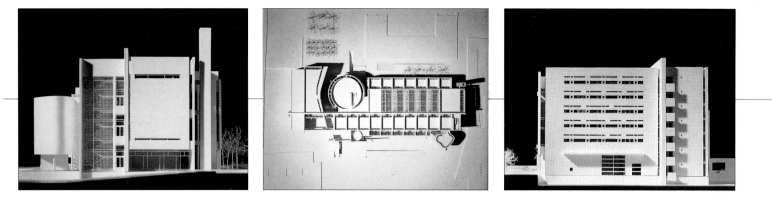

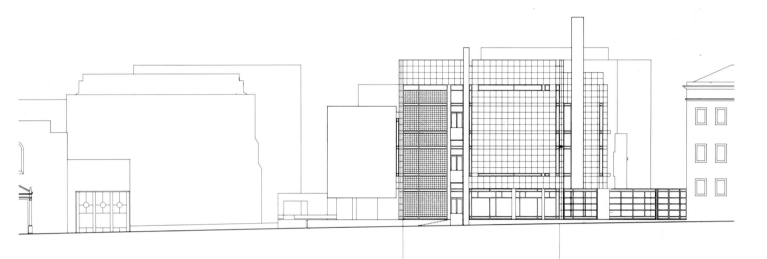

OPPOSITE PAGE: Second-floor and roof plans
ABOVE AND BELOW: Models of north-east
elevation, roof layout and south-west elevation,
graphic of east elevation, sections through east and
main galleries

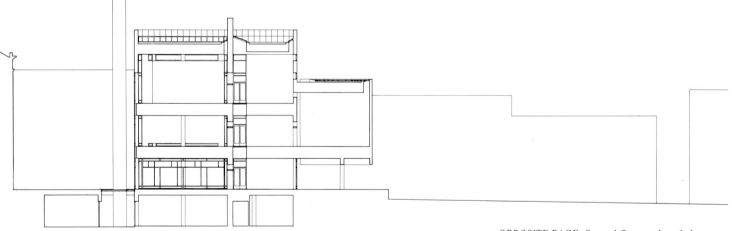

STEFANO DE MARTINO AND ALEX WALL
HOUSE FOR ZOE ZENGHELIS, LONDON

For an architect to create a home for an artist there has to exist a sensitivity and understanding. Architects Stefano de Martino and Alex Wall recently undertook the conversion of a traditional 19th-century house in London for clients Zoe Zenghelis and Peter Crookston. Zoe Zenghelis is an artist and one of the founder members of the Office for Metropolitan Architecture. She is well-known internationally for her architectural visions through her paintings, and runs the colour workshop at the Architectural Association. Her husband Peter Crookston is a journalist.

Architects de Martino and Wall write:
'The project consists of a reorganisation and extension. The reorganisation consists of repositioning rooms on different floors: the living spaces at ground level, the master bedroom suite on the first floor, the studio and guest room on the top floor. To maximise space in the garden flat and in the living room, the lower two floors were extended into the garden, adding a third layer to the 'back' and 'front' rooms. Correspondingly, a new light well was introduced at the rear.

'The extension of the house emphasises the linearity of the site, and the project effectively turns the rooms from being parallel to the street into spaces connecting the front of the house (street, city) with the back (garden, landscape), leaving the internal space poised between urbanity and a sense of arcadia.'

In the following *Architectural Design* interview, Zoe Zenghelis talks about the design and its relationship to her outlook on art . . .

– How did you come to choose Stefano and Alex?
I had been working together with Stefano and Alex at OMA. I think they are terrific designers and we also agree very much in terms of design and architecture. Therefore, we haven't had a single disagreement about anything.

– When did you decide to do the conversion?
I decided when I was going to marry Peter. I had already been living here for some 25 years. Rather than both of us looking for somewhere new to live we thought that it would be a better idea to work on this house, especially since we love the area.

– After choosing the architects, were you then involved much in the design of the house?
The way it worked out was that the architects suggested ideas and we would then discuss, and make changes or whatever. I was going to do the design myself, but thank God I didn't. First of all I would never have done as good a job as this and secondly having to deal with builders is terrible! You see, architecture has these wonderful moments of design and then, once you actually begin building, you have to become a referee, co-ordinator, lawyer, psychiatrist – even policeman!

– Did you initially give the architects a specific brief from which to work, or did you work on things as the designs were developing?
Well, at first the plan was to work on the basement of the house and create a two-room living space with a separate entrance from the rest of the house. However, the idea grew into working on the whole house, opening up the space.

– How were the materials chosen?
The materials were chosen by Stefano who would come up with two or three ideas and one would be decided upon. Often, the materials we were planning to use would lead to the choice of colours. For example, when the plaster was put in the house, I liked its colour so much that we found the same shade of paint to use on the living room and kitchen cupboards; and the plaster of the living room wall has been left unpainted – Stefano chose it for its colour. These two colours of plaster then led us to choose the beech plank floor for its soft pink colour.

– Having been involved in architecture for so long in your work, were there certain phases in the development of the architects' design when you became more critical than you might have been initially?
No. I have to say that at all stages I was very happy with the development of design.

– How did the techniques and themes in your painting influence the design you were looking for in the house?
Well, the other day someone came round who hadn't seen the house at all before and told me that it was like walking into one of my paintings.

– Yes, the colours are very similar. Did you have them in mind when planning the house?
Yes and often in painting even if I start with other colours I seem to eventually return to the same ones. Also the atmosphere here is very much the same as the paintings. The house has the same simplicity and a sort of minimalism.

– But would you call it a minimalist design?
I would say no. This design is not restrictive as minimalism can be. In this house, there is a freedom to put whatever you want in the space, and I think it still looks good.

– In your painting, you seek to evoke a certain mood, wanting the work to be suggestive of things rather than being something. Did you want to evoke a mood in the house?
Yes, unconsciously, I suppose. Even Stefano and Alex must have felt the same, given that they know me. The important thing is that we all know each other so well. We have worked together and appreciate one anothers' work; and now Stefano and I both teach at the Architectural Association. I like to think that there are different moods throughout the house as well and I definitely feel

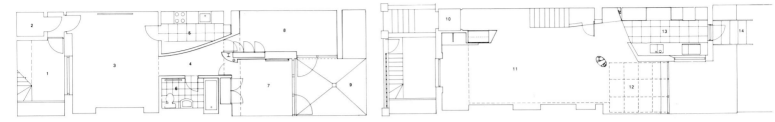

PREVIOUS SPREAD, LEFT, ABOVE, RIGHT, AND
OVERLEAF: Views of ground floor and plans of
basement, ground, second and third floors

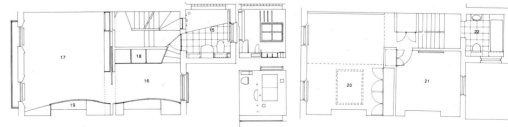

that built architecture can 'evoke' just as much as painting. A painting is not flat and you can walk into a painting as you can into a house (or a picture of a house for that matter!).

The bedroom, for instance, had to be left as it was apart from the cupboard which was a new design. And I think that the cupboard makes an issue and its shape evokes a mood. The idea was that I would make a mural on the cupboard; but I like it white, so I am in no hurry.

I wanted the living room downstairs to be very simple and have a space that would take anything. I find the cupboards in the kitchen important – being someone who does not like having things out, preferring to be able to finish with something and put it away, just leaving a surface, like the terrazzo top, which I designed myself, in the kitchen.

– *Have you done any paintings of the house, as you used to for OMA where you would make an abstract painting from the architectural plan?*

No I haven't, but if I did they would definitely be abstract. I don't do architectural paintings at all now, in the sense of working for specific designs. For me, architecture is a stage to painting. I use architectural signs as a way of developing analogies between space and forms. I like to poeticise the urban environment and I don't feel that my work imitates objective reality, but it is realistic enough to create a mood and an atmosphere. And though these moods such as sadness, emptiness and loneliness may be seen as negative, with my painting I try to turn them into something positive beautiful and seductive.

– *Do you look to Constructivism as much now as you used to in the past?*

Not so much. I find Constructivism fascinating with its use of geometry and proportions. But I find that atmospheric and emotional paintings have a longer life.

– *Does your visual sense as a painter allow you to better envisage a built work – the colours and forms in the house for instance?*

I suppose so; but don't forget that I have been working with architects over so many years.

– *Is the placing of paintings, furniture and objects in the house intrinsic to the design?*

There are really two households in this house and many of the paintings belong to my husband who likes collecting. There was a lot of thought towards how we could accommodate all the paintings he had in this space where walls are so important – the length of grey wall in the living room for example. Personally, I would prefer it to be completely empty, or just with panels of colours or extremely simple paintings. However, a house is a house with furniture and things you value and love around you, so what we have done is put my paintings, the palest ones, on the grey plaster wall so that they form part of the wall; but they can be replaced if I am exhibiting. I think this answers your question; everything moves around. Busy paintings, such as the ones Peter has, can go on the wall of the stairs, leading you upwards.

– *Finally, did you choose Stefano and Alex for their ideology?*

Yes, definitely. They are Modernists and I am sure that, if anything, they would like to be called Modern and nothing else.

STEFANO DE MARTINO
CHIAT & DAY OFFICES, LONDON

The offices for this advertising agency are located in the centre of London, a refurbished top floor and mezzanine level – a long, narrow area, beneath a barrel-vaulted roof, with views of the city on either side. The brief was to provide a workspace incorporating individual spaces, yet all existing in one environment with meeting rooms of various sizes close by.

The separate front and back views of this building were suggestive of the concept of our scheme. Therefore, we decided to highlight *sections* of the building rather than its overall length. Minimising the differences of opposing spaces became of paramount importance, and, to achieve this, we introduced three lines, to form three sections, which establish a link between north and south, upstairs and downstairs, small and large. Thus the first line deals with the office entrance, whilst the other two define the office spaces

and the double-height void. By virtue of cutting through the double height to single storey, different meeting situations are made possible: from informal to formal, and intimate offices to conference rooms. The double-height space is kept free as a reception area, serving as a 'public' space. The work sections follow a regular grid, interrupted by fibre-glass walls; and where these interruptions occur, exceptions are created in the workspace, rendering areas of interaction for everyone.

Architects: Stefano de Martino, Rem Koolhaas, DEGW Ltd; *Design team*: Stefano de Martino, Nick Boyarsky, Nicola Murphy, Simon Steel Hart, Tomas Quinjano (models); *Contractors*: Quickwood Ltd; *Furniture made by*: Terry Flowers (fibreglass), Jeremy Hughes (joinery and upholstery), David Racz, Mark Prizeman (metalwork).

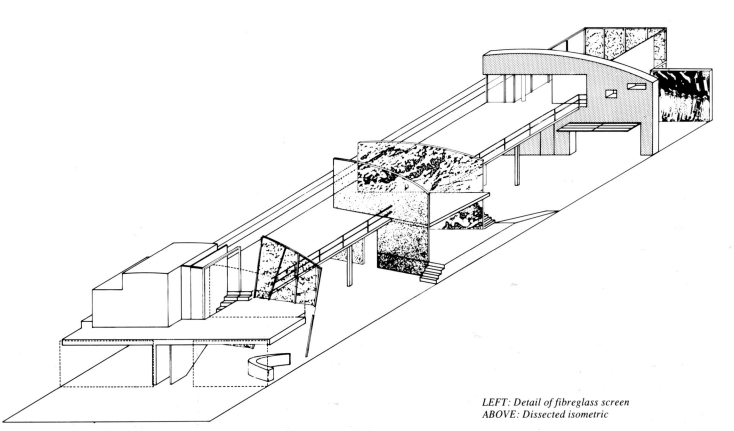

LEFT: Detail of fibreglass screen
ABOVE: Dissected isometric

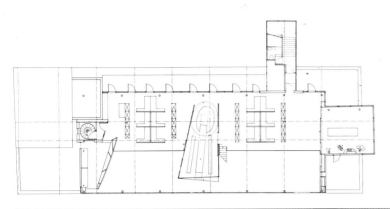

*LEFT: Reception area showing double-height void
ABOVE AND RIGHT: Meeting room with
conference table, and plans of mezzanine and top
floors*

LEFT: Central meeting room and 'amoebic'
fibreglass table
ABOVE AND RIGHT: Hydraulic picnic table over
'pit', and west and east elevations of central screens

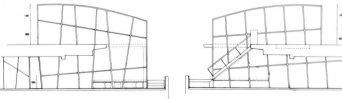

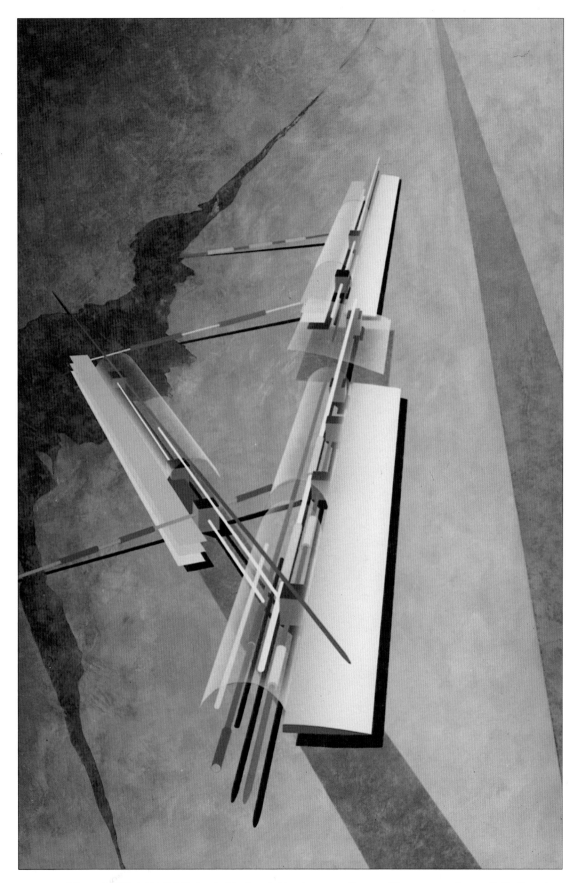

ODILE DECQ & BENOÎT CORNETTE, Apple Macintosh Headquarters, France. 'If someone tells you Odile Decq is a rock singer, don't believe it – she is an architect. But if someone tells you Benoît Cornette is a doctor, then believe it. A medical doctor, almost by chance has become an architect by his own will. The agency of these two odds, rewinded and animated with a serious swing, ends up being in rather good shape. In spite of their 'hard, black' look, they are easily happy. Mildness and tact has been their convincing trademark which made them become the craze of many financial clients from Brittany to Paris. From Bank branches (*Banque Populaire* and *Crédit Agricole* for example) to housing, a nursery school for the Poor Law Administration, they have done a good job.' *Philippe Tretiack*

YOUNG FRENCH ARCHITECTURE

After years of relative isolation, French architecture is now achieving widespread visibility once again, having been spurred on by the high level of public interest and national pride that has been generated by the *Grands Projets*. In spite of the fact that some of these, such as La Villette by Bernard Tschumi, and the Louvre Expansion by IM Pei have been more successful than others, and La Grande Arche of Tête Défense alone has managed the seemingly impossible feat of replacing l'Arc de Triomphe as a national monument, all of the 'Projects' represent a remarkable achievement. The governmental support making them possible has created a positive atmosphere that is perhaps rivalled only by Japan, in which architects now feel free to be innovative and iconoclastic and to explore new territory. As in Japan, much of this new architecture takes its cue from what Frédéric Borel, whose work is included here, has called the 'surface culture' induced by electronic proliferation, and the second industrial revolution of technology which is changing society so rapidly today. As with that culture, the stress in this new architecture is figurative communication, the message quickly sent to hopefully catch the attention of those scurrying down the boulevards, where *flaneurs* used to walk, or those racing down the highways to make the next appointment. Not all of the work shown here, however, is as transitory, presenting, more or less, a mirror image of the stylistic diversity represented by the *Grands Projets* themselves, albeit on a smaller scale. The evidence of this diversity begins with the Tacoma music store by Studio Naço, whose choice of a fast food favourite for a name begins to give some indication of their attitude to design. As with other architects, such as Nigel Coates, who seem to want to offset the temporal nature of certain projects, Studio Naço takes a 'total design' approach that typically includes furniture, graphics and lighting as well as the conformation of space.

Along with this commitment to become involved in controlling each aspect of the project, as well as the spatial experience that it provides, is an obvious awareness of the part that colour plays in the momentary urban encounters for which such space provides an analogue.

Rather than relying on stage-craft, Brénac and Gonzalez take a more traditionally Modernist line by playing materials off against each other but part company with the past in their joyful use of forms for their own sake, rather than as signals of the functions they introduce. While their architecture is undeniably descended from a Corbusian Machine Aesthetic, that aesthetic is elegantly, and richly, clad. They explore the tactile possibilities of juxtaposition, having a delicate glass window penetrate a massive granite wall in such a way that the inherent characteristics of each are exaggerated.

A similar love of the inherent qualities of materials is evident in the work of Martine Weissmann and Jean Léonard, who manage to evoke a sense of the momentous audacity involved in the Costes and Bellonte Paris-New York flight through their minimal use of stainless steel and grey granite. The strategic placement of metal and stone in their monument incongruously, but effectively, manages to express both the fragility of the plane and the drama of the event far better than any Hi-Tech wire act could possibly do.

Philippe Gazeau is equally concerned about such issues as the play of materials in his architecture, as well as to their appropriateness. His Cuisine Centrale shown here, which is clad in ribbed metal as befits its rather utilitarian purpose, is even more unabashedly Modernist in direction than the work of Brénac and Gonzalez, clearly recalling the Jugendstil planning techniques used so effectively in the brick houses designed by Mies Van der Rohe in 1923, where the walls seem to pinwheel out to infinity. While De Stijl principles are not employed as rigorously here, the linear heritage of the 'wallism' that Gazeau uses is unmistakable.

Walls also feature prominently in the Fréjus Necropolis by Bernard Desmoulin, which also displays great elegance in the handling of the materials used to build them. Instead of projecting into space however, the wall here is turned into a circle to create one of the most primal indications of a sacred 'place', which is used, in this case, as the burial ground for those killed in the Indo-China war. In a reminiscent of that used by Aldo Rossi in his Modena Cemetery project, Desmoulin uses Platonic geometry to set this place apart, and once having done so, builds his 'city of the dead' within it.

Such geometry is also evident in 'La Plus Petite Tour d'Europe' by architects Brunet and Saunier which is the most modest project included here, although the architects quote Jules Verne and Georges Meliès as sources. Rather than being brushed, as in the Costes and Bellonte monument, the stainless steel used to sheath this diminutive tower is highly polished, to both reflect its surroundings, and increase its scale.

Frédéric Borel's social housing project for Boulevard de Belleville also reveals an awareness of scale, but uses its brief as an opportunity to examine the present condition of a building type that has been much maligned recently. Following the social and economic debâcles of the post-war years in France, the latest renewal of interest in housing there has amounted to an act of courage by the public sector, and Borel's contribution here should be considered in that light.

It is rather appropriate that the last project to be included in this series, by Jean Robert Mazaud, should be the conversion of an industrial plant which brings this discussion back full circle to its technological beginnings. If nothing else, the *mélange* of directions shown here demonstrates the great variety, and vibrant good health, of French architecture today. *JS*

STUDIO NAÇO: TACOMA, NANTES

Tacoma is a project for a mega music store. We have designed everything from the architecture to the furniture, elevator and stairways, and from the lighting to the logo and graphics. We kept the two original walls and reconstructed the entire interior. The design of the space is seen as a whole where all components are related. We see the furniture as a piece of architecture that, at the same time, is tied to the graphic system with the use of an oval detail. The elevator tower is lodged in a deployed metal partition that creates an eccentric oval opening to floors above and below. The double stair is a flying carpet of metal and glass floating above its concrete base. The entire space is a rhythm of varied scales in the image of the universe of the city. The technical catwalk diagonally crosses the space to shelter the disc jockey cabin. It is a visual and sonorous sight. Colour is used as a signal. Metal runs throughout the space. A deployed metal roof protects the cash registers in the entry hall; the offices are located within a stainless steel submarine-like building. The design offers a transparency and dynamic graphic lines: a place of musical pleasure which favours communication between the levels and engages with the public.

OPPOSITE PAGE: Interior view
ABOVE, LEFT AND BELOW: Interior view, section and concept sketch

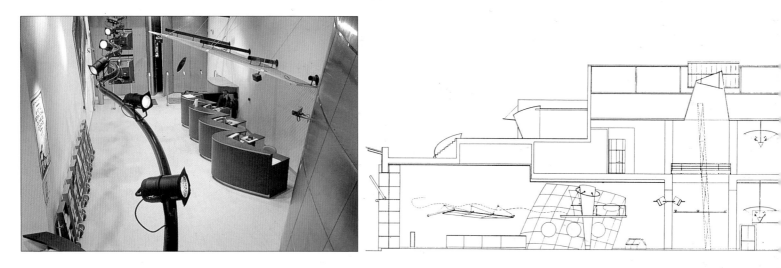

BRÉNAC & GONZALEZ: COLLEGE, PARIS
The college stands on the tip of a triangular site, two roads forking off on either side. The building takes its inspiration from the converging lines of both streets but in a staggered, displaced way. It forms a point, a prow of stone in layers.

The length of the converging facades are continual, clad in sanded or smooth stone – a rhythm of simple windows, slots and strips. On one side, a rhythm of lines and a sequence of volumes are achieved. On the other side, the streamlined curve of granite slides beneath the refined design of the facade.

'It is too early as yet to state that we have a "signature", but we do have principles. We always relate heavy masses with constructive lightness, as if weights were held from above, by beams, suspended in a void. We also like to utilise the play of double and triple heights.'

Inside, from the main hall, bathed in light, one can see the triple-levelled mezzanine. The library – the most public space – as well as the art and music rooms, are situated in the main building and open up above the entrance. On the other side of the hall are the classrooms each opening out onto the courtyard which is held between the two parts of the building.

OPPOSITE PAGE: Exterior views
ABOVE, LEFT AND BELOW: Exterior, interior and detailed views

WEISSMANN & LÉONARD: COSTES AND BELLONTE MONUMENT, SAINT-VALÉRY
The project was designed to commemorate the first Paris-New York flight, completed by pilots Costes and Bellonte on board their aeroplane 'Point d'interrogation'. The chosen site, the Saint-Valéry-en-Caux cliff, is the point from where the pilots had taken off, in September 1930. The monument is a beautiful, constructed object, which borders both sculpture and architecture. A monument is not an easy commission and the breadth of the surrounding cliff landscape complicated this task. They chose to underline, rather than mark, the monument, by a simple parvis of grey granite situated on the side of the cliff, reached by a series of steps. From there, one can look out onto an unobstructed view over the Saint-Valéry bay and the sea.

The monument itself is a discreetly narrative structure: two stainless steel walls cut through the space of the parvis. The bronze portraits of the pilots – two bas-reliefs – are embedded in the larger wall. The other recounts an adventure: an engraved aeroplane, another cut into the steel, and a wave symbolising the ocean the pilots crossed, together with engraved plans of the two cities and their emblems: the Eiffel Tower and the Statue of Liberty.

OPPOSITE PAGE: Detail of the monument
ABOVE, LEFT AND BELOW: Views of the monument and plan

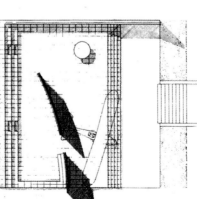

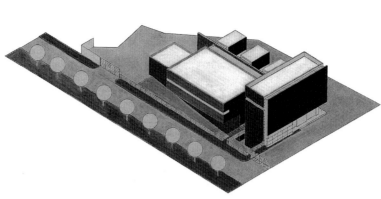

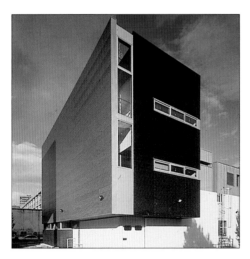

PHILIPPE GAZEAU: KITCHEN, PARIS

The brief for this building was to provide a central kitchen which would prepare meals to be sent out for schools, crèches and offices. 'An architect is at the heart of a paradox,' Gazeau has remarked. 'At the beginning of a project, he is the only one who knows nothing, whereas at the end he is the one who knows everything. He is the synthesis, the only person who can hold the thing together.' Whether he is building a kitchen, crèche or lycée, Gazeau employs a Corbusian stylistic, without making any concessions. Black and white, an architecture that is less Cubist perhaps than Pop art. The whole work is marked with force – punchy even. It is not by chance that one can witness the influence of Ciriani, as well as a fascination with conceptual American sculpture. From all this is born a vocabulary where simplicity, the 'less is more', and the minimalism of tools is accompanied by a clear brutalism.

ABOVE, LEFT AND BELOW: Interior and exterior views, axonometric and perspective

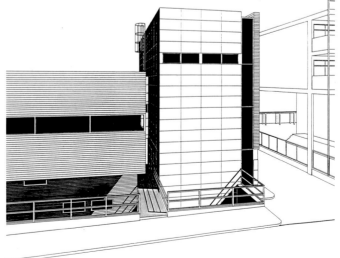

BERNARD DESMOULIN: NECROPOLIS, FRÉJUS

In 1987, a competition took place organised by the State Committee of War Veterans and Victims for the design of a national cemetery for the victims of the Indo-China war. The veterans chose a sloping site near Fréjus facing the sea. Even though the land is arid and bare, some parasol pines, olive and cypress trees grow in the area.

The town of Fréjus requested that 'a place' and not a field of crosses be constructed and, in this respect, Desmoulin's architectural language is completely innovative. Rather than lining up a series of crosses, he organised the cemetery into a large circle which formed a border and enclosure to the world. The circle is crossed by an axis the land gradient of which appears as a ramp receding towards Indo-China. The lines are sober and plain, as are the materials: ochre concrete, steel for the locks, and stone covering the ground.

The soldiers' funeral urns are aligned in a number of rows on the slope covering the crypt into which rays of sunlight penetrate.

ABOVE, LEFT AND BELOW: Detailed view, and site, crypt and upper-level plans

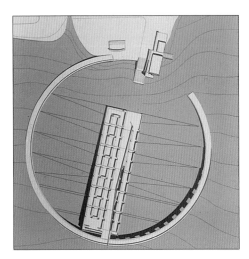

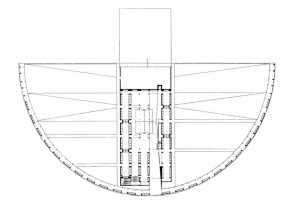

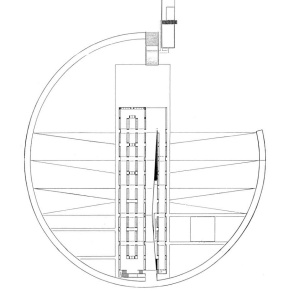

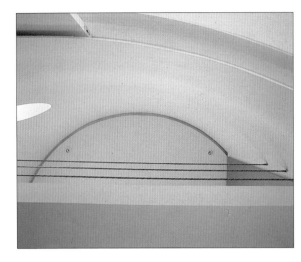

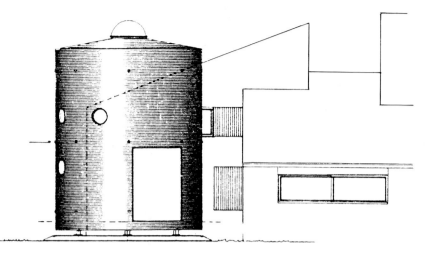

BRUNET & SAUNIER: THE SMALLEST TOWER IN EUROPE OR 'LE TOUR SANS FIN . . . ', HÉROUVILLE SAINT-CLAIR

The brief for this project had clearly defined parameters. The house was to be extended by one room, altering the existing building to a minimum and executed as cheaply and quickly as possible.

Directly derived from the 'Algeco' cabin or grain silo, the 'tower' alludes to Jules Verne and Georges Meliès. Constructed in wood and panelled in stainless steel, the building's exterior glimmers in its environment while, at the same time, it reflects its surroundings. The softly contoured, faded and hazily defined reflections bestow a dynamic impression upon the object, as if it were unceasingly turning – a tower 'touring' full circle, on the spot. Intended for the study and preparation of Baccalauréat exams, the tower houses a study on the ground floor and a bedroom on the first; suspended like a ring, floating in the volume of the cylinder: a suprasensorial coffer.

OPPOSITE PAGE: Exterior view
ABOVE, LEFT AND BELOW: Detailed interior and exterior views, elevation, dissected axonometric and site plan

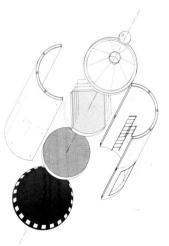

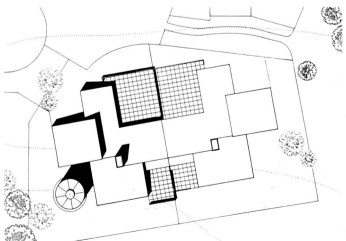

disconcerting in more ways than one. Modest in scale – 47 housing units – it is the work of 30-year old Frédéric Borel. Although the edifice does not call attention to itself, it poses a number of disturbing and perhaps essential questions for these tumultuous times.

The architect has turned the various constraints of the site to his advantage by means of a fragmented, skilfully articulated arrangement based on the architectural promenade, with gangways and footbridges, 'vistas' looking into the heart of the plot and a series of voids and solids (terraces) which together create a playful, joyous whole. The attention to detail, and the quality of execution in a wide variety of techniques, have something to do with the building's relaxed appearance and its lack of ostentatious display.

It retains our attention and is 'attractive' in its scenographic arrangement of detail, whether it be the spiral staircase jutting out from the rear facade, the chimney in the form of a richly detailed object, the languidly drawn-out scroll, or the gently undulating roof. On the boulevard – the public front – three sentinels stand on guard. The Spartan (or Iroquois) bowing to the city, the Samurai with his dark, metal corset, and Malevich's Moujik have somehow escaped from the Wizard of Oz: they salute the stroller, signal the building's presence and quietly pose the following, singular question: does figurative architecture exist? This suspicion emerged with Gaudí and the architectural expressionists. More recently, Japanese anthropomorphs and Venturian 'ducks' have furnished popular and reassuring examples. Here, however, the formal hints are infinitely more subtle and subversive and, presumably, of a quite different inspiration. Contemporary sensibilities are doubtless 'superficial', but they reflect what might also be termed 'surface culture' – a product of the video revolution and the cathode-ray tube. Procedures are multiple: delayed action, inversion, zoom and depth-of-field, fast and slow motion, montage and cut-up – a whole gamut of unheard-of (or rather, 'unseen-of') techniques.

Sooner or later, architecture will draw new inspiration from this 'surface culture' – in fact, the project seems to suggest this has already begun. Thus, construction will acquire a new sense of communication, a new lightness, and shake off a little of its high seriousness.
Olivier Boissière

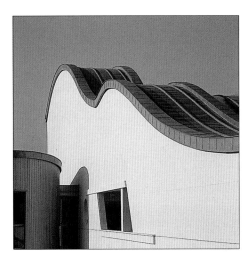

FRÉDÉRIC BOREL: HOUSING, PARIS
French architecture has woken up in two successive waves. During the 70s, angry young men bombed the Beaux Arts, debated and wrote manifestos, brandished the eternal question of the city and called to account the whole ossified profession. Although these architects matured, they were burdened with the conceptual framework they had built for themselves to prove they were operational.

The second generation is just hatching. It owes, to the first, a new-found freedom and access to commissions that suggest an architectural revival. Times have changed, however, as have sensibilities.

In Paris there exists a new building that is

OPPOSITE PAGE: View of entrance
ABOVE AND LEFT: Balcony, detailed and exterior views, and site plan

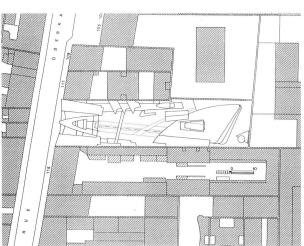

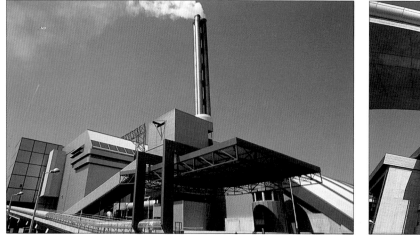

JEAN ROBERT MAZAUD: SAINT-OUEN II PLANT

In 1985, architects were challenged to transform the gigantic industrial machine that a domestic waste-disposal plant represents into an architectural creation of significance.

The controversy aroused by such an undertaking is understandable as there is an ambiguity between its functional necessity and image. We opted for an organic-mechanical model based on centralised symmetry, and plans were elaborated for a complex symbolising the controls of a living machine. Partly inspired by the workings of an enormous insect and partly by the mastery over fire, water and air, we designed forms which described climbing, gripping and rearing movements. The ramps wind into pincer-shaped volutes, the boiler room constitutes the encircled heart and is ringed by two clamp-shaped girders, the slag depot has the dual role of container and containment, the office block and its annexes glide forward, press against and enclose the complex, and the chimney soars up to form the town's distinctive landmark. It was important that technology should inspire the forms and that the spaces thus created, whether given to the plant or back to the town, should permit a communion between man and his environment.

OPPOSITE PAGE: Overall view
ABOVE, LEFT AND BELOW: Detailed and exterior views, and elevation

DUTCH RAILWAY STATION DESIGN

While the mere mention of a railway station usually conjures up visions of a grey, smoke filled, cavernous shed, the Dutch projects shown here represent a successful reversal of that old stereotype. This achievement is due, in no small part, to the enlightenment of Netherlands Railways Architects' Office who approached each project with the novel philosophy that the people who use the trains are more important than the trains themselves. Considering the passengers with a 'see and be seen' attitude, the designers sought to make each building a free-standing landmark that would delight the eye from the outside, and uplift the spirit within. Glass was the obvious choice of material to provide the kind of visibility that the architects wanted, and this transparency is consistently enhanced by vibrant colours and original works of art. The colours used are also cleverly coded to double as an information system with yellow linked with pedestrian routing, blue with waiting, red with structure and service and white as a reflector of light. Even the ever present problem of vandalism did not dampen the spirits of this group, who dealt with the pragmatics of that reality without allowing it to become an obsession. The result of all of these considerations is a joyful architecture of high quality, strong identity and great originality.

LEFT AND ABOVE: Harry Reijnders, Sloterdijk Station, Amsterdam, view of service column and overall exterior view

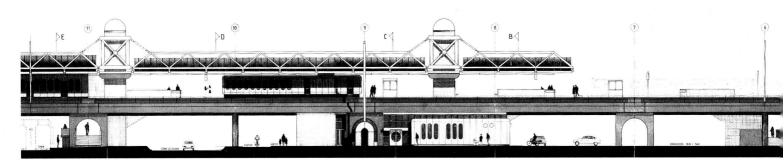

LEFT, ABOVE AND RIGHT: Rob Steenhuis,
Lelylaan Station, Amsterdam, view under canopy,
overall exterior view, elevation and sections

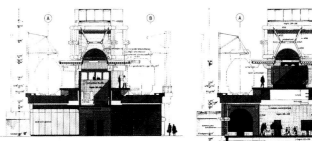

ABOVE AND BELOW: Peter van Kilsdonk, Almere Central Station, view of platforms and exterior view
ABOVE RIGHT AND RIGHT: Harry Reijnders, Leiden Central Station, view of model and elevation

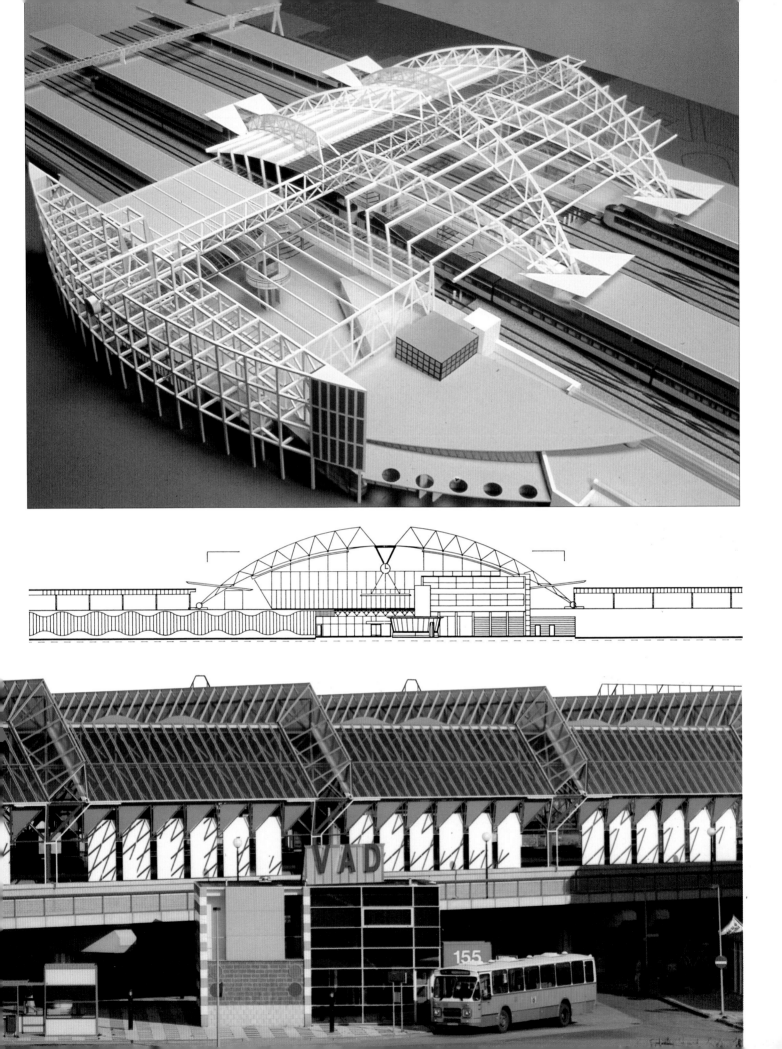

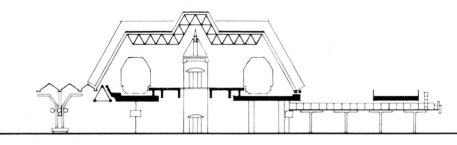

LEFT, ABOVE AND RIGHT: Peter van Kilsdonk,
Lelystad Central Station, view of atrium and
platform, exterior view and sections

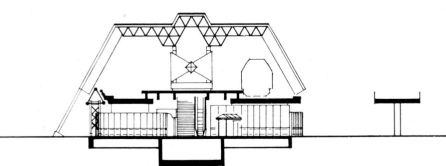

MARTIN PAWLEY
INFORMATION, THE 'GOTHIC SOLUTION'

Canterbury Cathedral from the south-west. Outrigged structure for free internal space – just like High-Tech.

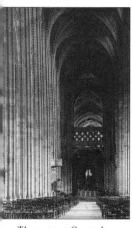

The nave at Canterbury. All the elements of the Gothic 'solar information system' brought together.

All a man needs in an office is a table and chair near a window and a few electric wires.
Quinlan Terry, 1988

In the last 15 years information has spread like a virus through the body of architecture. Unrecognised by most architects and ignored by most architectural historians and critics, it has changed its nature more radically than any technical or stylistic innovation since the advent of the Modern Movement. To find an equivalent period of information-driven change we have to go back more than 800 years to the boom in Gothic building that followed the rebuilding of the Benedictine Abbey of Saint-Denis near Paris by the Abbé Suger in 1144.

The idea of Gothic cathedrals as the historic predecessors of the paperless office and the electronic dealing room may at first seem surprising. This is because it is based upon an interpretation of the function of Gothic architecture that, to my knowledge, has no academic pedigree. Be this as it may, the parallel casts light on the ultimate architectural impact of the information revolution of the Second Machine Age.

There are many definitions of Gothic architecture. They range from structural and spatial analyses to abstract invocations of an ancient and inaccessible spiritual power. The most time-honoured definition is simply based on the presence of a unique structural feature, the ogival or pointed arch. In true Gothic buildings this arch formed the basis of a structural system in which repeated vaulting frameworks of intersecting stone ribs supported thin stone panels. The lateral and vertical loads carried by these complexes of vaults were collected and transmitted to the ground by means of rows of buttresses and flying buttresses. The presence of the ogival arch was the most obvious attribute of Gothic architecture, but this daring system of transmitting load was its essence, for it meant that the walls ceased to be loadbearing, and the window openings in them could be of unprecedented size.

This, in outline, is a description of Gothic architecture. But what is generally ignored in favour of an elaboration of these and other facts about it is what might be called its driving function. Clearly Gothic church and cathedral architecture was ecclesiastical in purpose, but what did the church gain from these structural *tours de force*, some of which were so ambitious that they actually collapsed and had to be built again or abandoned? The answer lies not in the spectacular daring of what was in effect the ultimate development of load-bearing stone construction, but in the information-carrying potential of the key design features that its unique system of transmitting loads made possible – great height and the giant window opening.

As the Gothic period advanced, increasing height and the enlargement of the openings in the curtain walls between the buttresses marked a steady development. Neither was merely an aesthetic device. The tall, thin acoustic space of the Gothic nave produced unprecedentedly long reverberation times[1] which responded to the sound of polyphonic chanting and choral music to produce an overwhelming aural effect. In the same way the windows ceased to be simple penetrations designed to admit light, but became instead complex translucent coloured-image screens built up from mosaics of stained glass. Coupled with the still astounding acoustic performance of these buildings, what remains of the imagery of their immense windows makes it clear that they were in fact total pre-electronic information systems.

In the context of feudal society, what we would now call the information content of the religious sounds and images of the Gothic cathedral was sufficient to explain its size and proportions – in exactly the same way as the demands of the electronic information technology of the modern financial services industry explain the column spacings and slab to slab heights of its buildings. Seen in this way Gothic architecture, otherwise a phenomenon shrouded in medieval mystery, becomes an information architecture, something that is comprehensible today, its great height and spectacular windows possessing a vital information function for mass congregations.

Inevitably the strength of any such analogy with the present depends upon the hypothesis that this teaching function was important enough to make it the driving force behind the extraordinary feats of Gothic construction. What proof is there that this might be the case? There is no documentary evidence, but modern acoustic measurement confirms that the exceedingly long reverberation times of Gothic cathedrals are inseparable from their height and shape and are only suitable for the kind of music that was made in them. In the same way the content and form of Gothic windows can be cited in support. First there is the indisputable information content of the medieval stained glass that survives, or can be conjectured from remains in the great cathedrals of Europe. Second there is the physical presence in these same buildings of precisely the kind of design detail that would emerge from the subordination of structure to acoustics and the display of immense naturally-lit images.

At Canterbury, the first complete English Gothic cathedral modelled on the French originals, and in fact designed by a French master, the clerestory windows of the choir running in a great band below the high vault clearly have a didactic purpose. They consist of an immense series of 88 images forming a family tree, based on the genealogy in St Luke's Gospel, from Adam to Jesus Christ. Of this series some 45 still survive. The great west window of the cathedral was too devoted to a 'teaching scheme'[2] including prophets, apostles and a series of 21 images of the kings of England from Canute to Henry VI, of which eight still remain. The fact that some of this stained glass is of a later date than the structure that surrounds it, of course in no way vitiates the theory that its insertion was the original purpose of the architecture.

In support of the second contention, that the primary function of the cathedrals was as supports for sound and vision, we have only to note that Gothic structure was outrigged – to use a modern term – while the interior surfaces of the window walls were flattened and cleared of projections in order to maximise the viewing angles to the window 'screens' and minimise any acoustic baffling effect that would have shortened the reverberation time. This is clearly functional design, and it is as logically expressed in the great Gothic cathedrals as it is in the lantern-lit roof structure of any art gallery today, or in the similarly uncompromising organisation of the information interior of any modern financial services building. The Gothic design imperative was the optimisation of its own 'vocal' and 'solar' information system based on naturally amplified sound and 'coloured light' filtered into the interior through large glass images.

At Chartres, the definitive Gothic cathedral described by Pevsner with an interesting choice of words as 'the final solution'[3] three-quarters of the original 13th-century glass has survived in 166 enormous windows devoted to narrative biblical themes. Here scholars do not dispute that the building's spectacular structure took the form it did in order to create huge wall openings. The elevations of the building comprise three storeys, but uniquely the arcade and the clerestory are of equal height and the gallery level is sacrificed in order to enlarge the window openings above it. These openings fill the entire space beneath the wall ribs.

Most dramatically in France, where Gothic architecture originated and underwent its most extreme development, but to a greater or lesser extent everywhere else in Europe, Gothic cathedrals and churches were public information buildings. Their huge windows were picture screens designed to use natural light to convey visual information to large numbers of people in a way that has no better equivalent than the projection of artificial light upon an image screen in the cinemas of the 20th century. And just as today there is no other explanation for the structure of a cinema auditorium than the functional demands of moving picture image projection for a large audience, so is there no better explanation for the structure and size of a Gothic cathedral than the functional demands of its information system.

It is perhaps appropriate at this stage to state the author's awareness that all the foregoing is a functional explanation for what is widely regarded as a spiritual, if not a mystical, phenomenon. The reader may feel that it hardly does justice to the polyvalent achievements of the Gothic masterbuilders, who repeatedly contrived to combine structure, decoration and information in an enormous single envelope with breathtaking clarity and daring. But it is as important to draw historical parallels where such are possible as it is to maintain a proper respect for the otherness of another age. The great Gothic cathedral stained glass windows, and indeed all their successors from the 12th century to the 19th- and 20th-century windows of Cologne, Truro and Coventry, are far more comprehensible as proto-photographic 'colour slides' in huge solar-lit 'projectors', with their own natural sound systems tuned by great height, than as abstract sculptures. The

design of Gothic cathedrals can be understood in the same way as the design of Frank Lloyd Wright's Guggenheim museum. Conceived in 1949 in the heyday of that other information building, the cinema, Wright's famous inset spiral glazing was derived entirely from an idea of natural light falling upon canvases inclined as upon an easel.[4]

Setting aside its spiritual purpose, the physical design of the information system of the Gothic cathedral can be related to the camera obscura, the magic lantern, the cinema projector, and today's exhibition designs that employ large numbers of illuminated transparencies or video walls. If its natural acoustic performance can now be duplicated electronically without the need for enormous structural height, so has the information content of its stained glass windows been miniaturised by the advent of moving pictures and analogue instrument displays, in which the same high density of information is presented, and indeed a kind of physical resemblance can be seen.

While the information system of the Gothic window was not electronic, it directed the development of Gothic architecture in precisely the same way as the diffused electronic information needs of our own time are directing the development of our own architecture. In the Gothic era the image was viewed direct and not electrically transmitted, so there was no cabling, ducting or heat output to consider in the design of church and cathedral buildings. Nonetheless the need for large images that could be seen by large numbers of people imposed its own spatial demands. Today the need for hundreds of individual visual information terminals leads to a different but analogous consumption of vertical and horizontal space in secular buildings. This is the best-known impact of information technology upon building design today, but its long-term consequence is underestimated. In fact it can be compared to the tip of an enormous iceberg that is threatening to tear through the flimsy hull that holds our thinking in thrall to the idea that the product of our built environment should still be architecture and not information.

Today, information about identity, where and where not to go, what to buy and what to think is no longer conveyed by form and appearance, as it might have been in the Gothic world. Instead a massive and separate semiological system has been overlaid upon the built environment. A visitor from Mars, asked to comment upon the architecture of the centre of Manchester for example, might well find the question bewildering. At the junction of the A56, A57 and A57M, adjacent to a bare half-dozen buildings there are, according to the Automobile Association, no less than 150 pieces of directional information, as well as advertising messages and shop or building names. To look at the buildings here instead of the signs requires a filtering out of a large part of the visual scene, and in performing that act of filtration an involuntary censorship of the real world takes place.

Seen in this way, even the journey from the Gothic cathedral to financial services building is not impossible to imagine; and from the twinkling VDUs of the dealing room to the macro-signage of the motorway intersection, or from there to the micro-signage of our newspapers and magazines is but a step. In all these cases a process of selective perception is what makes the environment intelligible. If we cease to make even as simple a distinction as that between advertising and editorial material in a magazine we fall into a chaotic world of simultaneous information transmission. The effect is rather like looking at – instead of filtering out – the invasion of information that has taken place in sport

19th-century reproduction Gothic window at Cologne Cathedral. A figurative 'narrative slide show'.

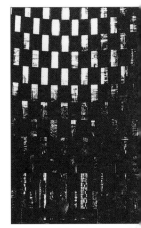

20th-century John Piper Baptistery window at Coventry Cathedral. On the way from narrative to digital information by way of abstract art.

Even cheap information beats expensive architectural form as a conveyor of meaning in the environment.

The A320 Airbus, the first airliner with fully integrated video displays. Not that far from Piper's window at Coventry.

Final disconnection of external form from internal function. The old Mary Pickford film studios at Baldock, Herts, now a superstore behind the studio façade.

Richard Horden, Stag Place competition project, 1987. But the dramatisation of electronic antennae will not prevent somebody else from hiding them under a dome.

under the name of sponsorship; with not merely every Grand Prix racing car plastered in commercial messages, but even the surface of the drivers' racing overalls and helmet rentable for advertising purposes.[5] To object that this process is unimportant invites the question: 'Unimportant to whom?' For just as there would be no economic flow of traffic through Manchester without the forest of signs, so would there be no Grand Prix superstar drivers if they were not allowed to market the very clothes they are strapped down in.

What we have in the modern world is a disorganised multiplicity of sign systems tracking back through time, of which perhaps the oldest and most overlaid is architecture. The incompatibility of these superimposed systems is resolved today only by the filtering effect of our own educated perception which, in turn, is increasingly faced with the prospect of being overwhelmed. The audible stall warning directed to an airline pilot, for example, is there because his capacity to receive visual information is already overloaded. If the pilot of a 150-ton airliner with 500 persons on board travelling at 500 miles an hour requires compressed, intensified and analytical information – a kind of digitised Gothic window in fact – so do we, the inhabitants of a rootless, fragmented, fast-moving sensory world of signs and symbols, require an integrated 'information environment' that is more efficient than a background of applied architectural styles plastered with messages.

It is the lesson of the great Gothic information system that this present state of wasteful and confusing information redundancy need only be temporary. Notwithstanding the rearguard actions of conservationists and aesthetic speculators today, the built environment will not continue indefinitely to make only grudging and specialised adjustments to the radical imperative of information. Our much-criticised environmental disorder may indeed only be a consequence of the dominance of obsolescent and redundant thinking on this subject in institutions and academies. It is only because we lack the perspective of centuries that we cannot see the 'Gothic solution' that is already emerging in our midst. If the cathedral master builders found an architecture that completely expressed the information content of their culture, *mutatis mutandis* so can we. If the Gothic analogy is correct, the next step in architecture should be a reintegration of the built environment with the overlaid information systems that have been allowed to take over its proper task.

'It is unfortunate,' wrote the architect Theo Crosby in 1987, 'that technology turned out to be such a slippery little beast, rapidly changing from a solid Victorian machine aesthetic into a bundle of wires and chips.'[6] Crosby was writing about the information revolution, something that in the last decade has brought about a massive shift from an industrial economy to an information economy. As de Marillac has observed,

> While we have paid lip service to the 'Information Age' for years, we have never really understood its consequences and still do not admit its reality. The increase in the rate at which money is being earned for our national enterprises by machines manipulated by information, rather than tended by men and women, is having a far greater effect than we realise.[7]

Accurate though he was, Crosby was late with his observation. 20 years earlier, in a remarkable insight, the American architect Edgar Kaufmann Jr saw this same revolution not as the dissolution of a technology, but as proof of the arrival of an era of disposability – or 'ephemeralisation', to use a Buckminster Fuller word. 'Technology is increasingly immaterial,' wrote Kaufmann in 1966, 'it is increasingly electronic, less mechanical, and the net result is that the imagery of technology readily eludes the designer.' But Kaufmann did not see this elusiveness as a reason to give up the hunt for the face of technology. He saw a new quarry in 'disposable buildings', conceived for a new economy that finds value

> not in the object, but in how people think about it, how they get it to you, and what you can do with it . . . Within the great impersonality of the world of mass production and near-disposability (he wrote prophetically) there becomes clear for the first time the possibility of an intense personalism as a proper balance and as a proper enrichment of life. The future of design lies in situation design and not in product design; products merely implement the situations.[8]

Because it consists of capital-intensive, decentralised installations – not concentrated objects of public spectacle – the apparatus of the information economy has become miniaturised, privatised and concealed. For architecture this has resulted in a changed perception in which the old technology of industry has lost all cultural value. Rightly or wrongly it is no longer a source of creative inspiration. Even where, as in the case of the motorway network, it is ubiquitous and impossible to ignore, the industrial infrastructure is seen by most architects as an alien force to be fought off and delayed or diverted by local enterprise. The architectural politics generated today by the ephemeralisation that Kaufmann and Crosby identify is intensely reactionary. Instead of looking forward to ephemeralisation, it fights a rearguard action against machines. And even where they are invisible – as the machinery of information truly is – it conceals them within an antique shell.

The consequent final disconnection of external form from internal function is the one architectural event of historic significance that can truly have been said to have taken place in the 1980s. It marks the final shift from an industrial economy to an information economy, a dislocation that is epitomised by the international computerised micro-copying facility that is operated by monks inside the walls of the sixth-century Abbey of Saint-Wandrille in Northern France[9] – and the laborious consultation of bound ledgers by as yet uncomputerised underwriters in the space age surroundings of the new Lloyd's building.

The post-industrial economy operates without an affirmative architecture of its own. Largely as a result of the technical achievements of the First Machine Age, its primary energy is no longer provided mechanically but electrically generated with the aid of invisible fuels from North Sea oil platforms over the horizon, ominous nuclear power stations located on deserted stretches of coast, or arriving by submarine cable from mainland Europe. Most of its exports are no longer manufactured goods, but formless liquid fuels, chemicals and invisible credits. Even the shrinking proportion of trade that is in manufactures consists of containers craned, trucked and shipped between anonymous depots. Most important of all, the largest single business of the post-industrial economy, the buying and selling of houses, is a financial rather than a productive process that favours scarcity. Expensive houses that appreciate in value like works of art call for embellishment rather than simplification. A successful marketing strategy for them requires special design skills, not only beneath the threshold of architectural significance established by the Modern era, but irrelevant to the design of fast-depreciating industrial and commercial buildings.

Of course there have been palaces purpose-built for the green-screen jockeys of the new information economy, but these present an enigmatic exterior that masks their exciting inner world. Reactionary architectural culture finds them unsatisfactory and requires them to look either like old photographs or, more correctly, collages of old photographs using historical architectural motifs in unhistorical ways. The result of this restriction is an architecture of illusion whose deficiencies can really be understood only by those who actually work in the information economy. Unlike outside observers, they daily experience the lack of any connection between their flight deck-style work stations and the external appearance of the buildings that house them, whether they be the science park sheds in which they work, or the ornate, brick-skinned timber-frame houses they live in. The new information workers can see, popular opinion to the contrary, that their labour does not presuppose the need for anything like the lavish structural expressionism of the Hong Kong and Shanghai Bank or the Lloyd's building – even though both were designed with the dedication, if not the ultimate success, of a Gothic master builder.

So far, far from giving rise to a new aesthetic, the information economy has presented the architects of today's banks and offices with a new and formidable variant of the problem that confronted the architects of yesterday's giant cinemas. The 992-line video screen, like the 35-mm moving picture frame, has no implicit architecture. Apart from the size of its auditorium, even the development of a recognisable international style for the cinema – which was achieved in the 1930s in the guise of a 'picture palace' – was a matter of historical analogy rather than functional logic. Its recognisable international form was destined to last a bare 20 years before it was rendered obsolete by the powerful decentralising force of television and video.

Where Victorian communications technology brought forth mighty ships, huge bridges, viaducts and giant railway stations – and even Victorian information technology demanded extravagant daylighting and the capacity to handle a huge tonnage of books, paperwork and personnel – today's electronic communications operate through satellite links whose visible impact on building design need be no greater than the presence of a dish aerial on the roof and work stations on the open-plan office floors. Even the concealed 'supply side' space demands of new technology are now generally agreed to be matters of internal arrangement rather than excuses for 'bowellist' formalism.[10]

Thus the high-tech bid to express service functions as though they were structure has imploded in the vacuum of ephemeralisation. While it might be all very well to expose toilet modules, escape stairs and glittering service trunking; coaxial cables, fibre optics, lasers and infra-red signals need easy access and a controlled climate rather than a system of display. And while it is true that they cannot be too savagely kinked as they squirm their way past columns or under floors, their architectural implications are better dealt with by specialist engineers – even specialist cabling engineers – than by architects.

Where there is no overwhelming constraint on space, information already prefers to navigate a received world of buildings that have already been designed. Its technologists ask for nothing more than that the architect should be off the case before they get to work. Typically an expert cabling company representative writes in *The Architects' Journal*: 'Virtually the whole project was run by technolo-

gists and bank staff. Had it been left to the architects, this building would have been a disaster. They think information technology is a small branch of mechanical and electrical servicing.'[11] As long as this 'no-nonsense' thinking is dominant at the point of sale, we can be sure that architects will not be encouraged to enter the field of information technology at all. Apart from the need to 'leave room' for it, architects are supposed to concentrate on other things.

But what other things are there? In the age of the messenger with a letter, information meant keeping messengers, and their horses, alive as they relayed across the country: today, information means codes and images that inhabit their own world within buildings, within cars, even within pockets or wristwatches. From a bare trickle of hand-written documents passed down from generation to generation – philosophers 'talking across the centuries' – information has become a roaring tide that fills the very air we breathe. Put up an aerial wherever you are and you have information; open your eyes and you have images that you cannot escape.

Most architects, even those who are successful in achieving massive image replication for themselves, are unaware of the huge scale of this image cascade, or of the irrelevance of any theoretical position they may profess to hold to their performance within it. A successful late 20th-century architect may try to externalise a form from the formless technologies that have ephemeralised his art, for instance by seeking inspiration in those few incontrovertible structural demands that the information economy does make. The need to support microwave and satellite antennae, for example, was heavily dramatised in the original winning design by Richard Horden for the £30 million Stag Place competition of 1987 – even though much publicity about the miniaturisation of dish antenna technology coincided with the publication of his scheme. In the same way the ostentatious expression of all the equipment needed to maintain the exacting indoor environment required by information processing machines provides part of the rationale for the 'inside out' appearance of the Lloyd's building.

Though often praised in professional magazines, this 'loyal functionalism' is in reality little more than a pathetic cargo-culting of the lost methodology of the Modern era. No burden of antennae, however vastly exaggerated, and no tonnage of climate control can make sufficiently challenging formal demands to determine incontrovertibly the design of a new building in the way that the mighty Gothic window did for the medieval master builder. On the contrary, these new electronic 'functional demands' can be hidden with equal ease behind mirror glass or Classical façades. The rapidly miniaturising dish aerial can already be lost inside a Renaissance dome, the climate control equipment immured in a blind-windowed antechamber.

Julian Bicknell, the architect of one of the most elaborate Classical Revival buildings in Britain, the celebrated £2 million Palladian villa built for Sebastian de Ferranti at Henbury, near Macclesfield, argues that in this respect information technology today is so far ahead of architecture that it is laughable to imagine that architects should try to encompass it at all. How much more sensible, he believes, to take a fully developed set of old ideas, like Classical architecture, and use them instead.[12] Such an approach is after all much in the spirit of 'information'. In the present state of architecture it is not only more sensible but, we are assured, more rewarding to 'plug-in' to what

The evolution of the 'Gothic solution' I. Mies Van der Rohe's Farnsworth House of 1948. Note the terrace sculpture.

The evolution of the 'Gothic solution' II. Esso petrol station at Heston on the M4, 1988. Note the vent pipes.

The evolution of the 'Gothic solution' III. I M Pei, Hancock Tower, Boston 1970.

The evolution of the 'Gothic solution' IV. Tenterden Street, CMW Architects, 1987. Take Mies and marry it to a curve.

The evolution of the 'Gothic solution' V. Ludgate House, Fitzroy Robinson, 1989. Small, but almost the perfect architecture of the information age.

Montgolfier hot-air balloon, 1783. An old answer, but a good one, to decorate with a low coefficient of drag.

another Classical Revival architect, Robert Adam, has called 'the great battery of Renaissance architecture from which we can all recharge ourselves at will' than to go on stubbornly turning the key of functionalism on the flat battery of Modern architecture.

In fact to argue that the expression of any architectural style should have precedence in design over information itself is as futile as arguing the superiority of a 'Heritage' Morris Minor over a new BMW saloon. A restored Morris Minor may be an appreciating asset, but it is no more a useful tool today than a manual typewriter. A new BMW is not only a useful tool but one that is poised (in the midst of the information revolution) to build a bridge between the home and the work station by way of its own burgeoning information technology. A comfortable 130 mph car with a computer terminal and a telephone is, after all, a serious threat to architecture. As the advertisement says, 'With a car like this who needs an office?

In fact the role of a typewriter salesman in a paperless office is very similar to the role of even a 'high-tech' architect in a world overwhelmed by information. Because information is an ephemeralised commodity the architect cannot relate the physical appearance of his building to its physical functions except by extravagant metaphor. At the same time the confusing message of the image cascade is that he can – because an appropriate form language does exist, in the shape of the architectural equivalent to the BMW saloon, itself perhaps the 'Gothic solution' to the problem of the design of the automobile. Indeed it is true that where massive amounts of information have to be crammed into tiny spaces, as on the flight deck of an airliner, or behind the fascia of a modern car, the beginnings of an information architecture can be seen. But where information can still be crammed invisibly under the floor, or tacked in wires around the walls, the case is hopeless. Today the high-tech architect must pitch his would-be BMW building against the Morris Minor-with-a-telephone of the Classical Revivalist, and in doing so he invites defeat because he is still thinking in terms of architecture and not information.

Today a building bereft of information is dead, whatever its period. Just as a garage is a building without purpose if there is no vehicle to store in it because the two are symbiotic – so is the modern dwelling, like the modern office building, a dinosaur without electronic information. Information, and information alone, holds the key to investment; it is the card that trumps the building bureaucracy, the *bona fides* of undisputed importance. Where discussions about style flounder and degenerate into tiny power struggles between would-be critics of architecture who are graduate geographers, and would-be architects who have been trained for nothing but architectural criticism, the cables, beams and dishes of information sweep through without impediment.

What, for example, determines the appearance of a petrol station – a building type in which information and architecture are already as nearly perfectly integrated as in a Gothic cathedral? The prototype petrol station is Mies Van der Rohe's Farnsworth House of 1948, with the addition of information and energy. Energy in the form of millions of gallons of motor fuel, information conveyed in signs so detailed that they not only carry unit prices down to tenths of a penny, but can be altered instantaneously by a modem call from hundreds of miles away. Petrol stations, colour-coded in the livery of their parent oil company, are buildings made of information, clad in signs that range from

their giant illuminated roadside towers to the crucial price and quantity information on the petrol pumps themselves.

Semiological robot buildings like the petrol station are one indicator of the road that unimpeded information technology would push architecture down. Another is the way that, as we have seen, it will determine the distance between the floor slabs of a modern multi-storey office building, and the resultant system of raised floors, false ceilings and risers to provide space for cabling and ducting will determine not only the storey heights, but the overall height of the building relative to its floor area, and thus its commercial value too.

It is here, at this final non-creative level of ruthless objectivity, that the shape of a new 'Gothic solution' for the age of information finally becomes visible against the camouflage of the Heritage environment. For just as the functional demands of the stained glass information system created the outrigged structure and internal space of the Gothic cathedral, so have the demands of the world of electronic information already laid an irresistible hand upon the form of the buildings of the Second Machine Age.

Eight hundred years ago, when Gothic structure was 'dematerialised' by the need for light, the residual structural mass that held up the windows had its own information function too. The walls, towers, spires, buttresses, arches and reveals of the great cathedrals were all made to carry information in the form of sculptures and low reliefs. Because of the quantum of effort involved in carving these friezes and effigies, we can be sure that they were not afterthoughts of the cathedral builders. Nor were they the result of an indiscriminate process of ornament that sought to decorate every available surface. There are bare and functional surfaces on the exteriors as well as the interiors of Gothic cathedrals; the sides of the buttresses and their included curtain walls; the slopes of their steeply pitched roofs and the upper surface of the copings designed to protect exposed edges from weathering, all these were left bare for reasons of sound construction practice. The massively decorated external surfaces of the Gothic cathedrals were those exposed to ceremonial public view.

It is this final parallel that enables us to complete the specification for a new 'Gothic solution', for it shows us how the new information buildings of the Second Machine Age can be physically bland but informationally 'decorated'. Externally their structural frame or monocoque skin will be rationally and economically designed by engineers to support a vertical sandwich of alternate service zones and occupied areas. Internally the relative volume of these zones will be flexible, and their arrangement will be governed by present and anticipated space and climate control needs. Though the height of these buildings will range from one to 100 storeys or more, this arrangement will be standardised. In general, compared to the buildings of today, the structural floor-to-floor heights of these buildings will be greater, and their climate control systems more powerful and adaptable: if necessary their cooling systems will be able to absorb very large electrically generated heating loads. Irrespective of their height, the occupied space in these buildings will be located between accessible service zones that permit rapid reconfiguration without internal disruption. In taller buildings, personnel movement will be by escalator, and goods transport will be by lifts that stop at service floors as well as people-floors. Within the occupied areas there will be flexible partitioning systems that also provide for rapid reconfiguration, like the seating arrangements in an airliner. The envelope enclosing these sandwich buildings will be a thin, high-performance glass, ceramic or metallic skin of minimum surface area. The roof will either be flat and waterproofed with a single synthetic membrane laid over such insulation and structure as is necessary, or be part of the same curvilinear envelope as the walls.

This building is the new 'Gothic solution', and of course this description is an anticlimax because, in part, it is immediately recognisable. With the exception of a few details, many buildings answering this description already exist and are in daily use, while others exist in the form of projects. The smooth outer cladding of the frame version is already a common sight in most North American cities. In England most of its features can be discerned at Ludgate House, the 10-storey office block at Southwark Bridge by Fitzroy Robinson, completed in 1989. But its origin lies much further back. With the exception of the latest information technology, nearly everything is in place in the Willis Faber & Dumas insurance office building in Ipswich, designed by Norman Foster in 1972. Before that, the basic arrangement without the smooth cladding that became possible with gasket glazing is present in the later commercial designs of Mies Van der Rohe, notably the unbuilt 1967 project for Mansion House Square in the City of London, and the posthumously completed IBM tower in Chicago. The earliest versions of this, in turn, can be seen in the work of Erich Mendelsohn in Germany and the Czech functionalist architects in Prague during the 1920s. The very first coherent image of the 'Gothic solution' can be glimpsed in the two projects for glass skyscrapers that Mies Van der Rohe drew as long ago as 1919. Before that, its key components must be sought separately in the 19th-century development of the frame building, the hydraulic lift and electricity.

What we have described above is a commercial building, but all the elements of the 'Gothic solution' will eventually migrate to the farthest corners of the built environment. The first domestic raised floor will follow the 'worktop', the lighting track and the 'technology beam' from the office equipment catalogue into the living room, just as the steel frame structure leaped from the factory, to the office, to the house. The combination of elements that the 'Gothic solution' has patiently assembled over the last 70 years is already as potent a precursor as the Abbey of Saint-Denis. It is the solution to all the problems of accommodating the age of electronic information except one – the 'cultural' problem of individual creativity, the old 'survival function' of the profession.

As the single most important contributor to the evolution of a multi-functional 'Gothic solution' architecture, Mies Van der Rohe understood this. Earlier than any other architect he faced the fact that the new age 'Gothic solution' building was destined to lack physical art-historical features. For Mies Van der Rohe to design a house, a factory and an office block in the same way was an achievement whose radicalism is clearer to us after the fall of Modern architecture than it was to his contemporaries.

Even today such buildings look like popular magazines with blank covers, or Grand Prix racing cars devoid of sponsorship. Their smooth glass and metal skins convey no comforting historical message. Mies Van der Rohe came to terms with this anonymity during his long career. 'I believe that architecture has little or nothing to do with the invention of interesting forms or with personal inclinations,' he said towards the end of his life. 'True architecture is always objective and is the expression of the inner structure of our time.[13]

But Mies Van der Rohe was not destined to see the final achievement of the 'Gothic solution'. In his greatest buildings there is an inevitable emptiness that cannot by any stunting of the imagination be compared to the multivalent visual impact of the Gothic façade. His 'objective' architecture made plain the unbridgeable gap that exists in reality – and cannot be closed by sentimentality – between the small, close-knit, interdependent society of the feudal age, and the vast, atomised, material culture of the 20th century. But even his material culture was smaller and less attenuated than ours, for it had not yet come to electronic life. Mies Van der Rohe refused to obscure nothing when nothing was what there was. In one sense this is why his greatness can still illuminate the floundering sentimentality of the present. Better by far for the conscientious objectors of the Second Machine Age that the real world of information should be concealed behind some laboriously modelled Dickensian street façade, than that they should see the bland, glass elevations of the 'Gothic solution' as they are – no more empty than a video screen, or a Gothic window.

Consider the enormous surface area of the 'Gothic solution' building alongside the equally bland and enormous envelope of a blimp. Structurally the building better resembles a rigid airship, but such vessels died out 50 years ago, and we are left today with the smaller non-rigid, a pale shadow of its great ancestor. Like the blimp and the rigid airship, and indeed like the hot-air balloon and all balloons going back to the original Montgolfier, like the skeleton of the Gothic cathedral or the stark structure of the petrol station, the vast, flat surface of the electronic information building is a canvas crying out to be bathed in colour and sound.

Just as the blimp became a vehicle for advertising, droning over the city at night using its streamlined surface to perform illuminated graphic tricks, so will the cathedral of information, the new 'Gothic solution', give up the unequal battle with art-historical architecture's 'vertical posture, articulation through detail and light and shade',[14] and paint its face with electronic images instead. It can do this. It can do it now. Only one thing stands in its way: the obsolete notion that, because it is architecture, it must convey a distinctive visual message through its permanent physical form. The golden age of the 'Gothic solution' will begin with the conquest of this last illusion of architectural history.

The evolution of the 'Gothic solution' VI. Future Systems: 'The Blob' 1987. Its space-efficient surface electronically informationalised, this will be the 'Gothic solution' of the 21st century.

Future Systems: premiated Paris Bibliothèque Nationale competition entry, 1989.

The Crystal Palace, 1851, Sir Joseph Paxton's pre-emptive masterpiece of component design and project management.

This feature is an extract from the book Theory and Design in the Second Machine Age *by Martin Pawley, published by Basil Blackwell, Oxford and reproduced here by kind permission of the publishers.*

1 The optimum reverberation time for audible speech is of the order of 1.3 seconds. A modern concert hall might ideally have a reverberation time of two seconds. A Gothic cathedral commonly requires more than six seconds for sounds to decay. All these parameters can now be changed electronically, without the need for physical changes in building form.

2 This term is used by Canon Ingram Hill in his description of the stained glass at Canterbury, see The Revd Canon D Ingram Hill, *Canterbury Cathedral*, Bell & Hyman, 1986.

3 'France moved on, from the Early to the High Gothic, in a growth from cathedral to cathedral until the master of Chartres *found the final solution*', see Nikolaus Pevsner, *The Cathedrals of England*, Viking, 1985, (italics supplied).

4 For an account of the design ideas behind the Guggenheim, see Brendan Gill, *Many Masks: A Life of Frank Lloyd Wright,* Heinemann, London, 1988.

5 'It used to be that a Grand Prix driver's overalls were just a first-line defence against fire. Nowadays, brandishing the right badges on a triple-layer Nomex suit is the cornerstone to a million-dollar lifestyle', *Motor*, 20 July 1985. This remarkable unsigned article on Grand Prix sponsorship details the breaking down of the upper part of the racing driver's overalls into rentable spaces and the rationing of these spaces in advertisements by the use of permitted camera angles and picture cropping.

6 Theo Crosby, *Let's Build a Monument*, Pentagram, 1987.

7 M de Marillac, 'Pioneers in a Jobless Society', *The Times*, 11 May 1987.

8 Edgar Kaufmann Jr, 'Design, sans peur and sans ressources', *Architectural Forum*, September 1966.

9 Roger Beardwood, 'Between God and Mammon', *Business*, May 1987.

10 'Bowellism' was the term originally used to describe Michael Webb's design for a furniture manufacturer's headquarters at High Wycombe. This scheme, with its exposed servicing elements, was a distant (1959) ancestor of the Lloyd's building, and a seminal influence on the Archigram Group.

11 'Cabling Guide, Part 5. Future Imperatives', Eosys Ltd, *The Architects' Journal*, 6 July 1988, p 54. The author too has been thus advised by senior executives at Hoskyns plc, a specialist information technology installation firm. 'The intelligent building is nothing to do with the property it lives in,' he was told by one senior engineer. 'Whatever the building is like, you will always be able to shoe-horn the stuff in.'

12 In conversation with the author during 1987.

13 Quoted in Peter Carter, *Mies Van der Rohe at Work*, Praeger, 1974.

14 These are the 'three principles of architecture that we must get back to', according to Roger Scruton in a talk he gave at the RIBA in April 1983 based on his book *The Aesthetics of Architecture*, Methuen, 1979.

INTERNATIONAL FURNITURE FAIR

1991
26ᵗʰ SEPT. - 1ˢᵗ OCTOBER
VALENCIA - SPAIN

I28 FERIA·
INTERNACIONAL
DEL MUEBLE

IBERIA IB ICEX   GENERALITAT VALENCIANA

DIMARC

ARCHITECTURAL DESIGN

1990 ANNUAL SUBSCRIPTION RATE (for six double issues inc p&p) *Architectural Design*, UK only £49.50. Europe £59.50. Overseas US$99.50. Reduced Student Rate: UK £45. Europe £55. Overseas US$89.50. Subscriptions may be backdated to any issue.

... 1 ARATA ISOZAKI
    0 85670 330 3   £3.95

... 3 TAFURI/CULOT/KRIER
    0 85670 355 9   £3.95

... 4 POST-MODERNISM
    0 85670 356 7   £3.95

... 11 SURREALISM
    0 85670 409 1   £6.95

... 14 HAND-BUILT HORNBY
    0 85670 430 X   £3.95

... 16 BRUCE GOFF
    0 85670 432 6   £6.95

... 19 SAINSBURY CENTRE
    0 85670 563 2   £3.95

... 20 ROMA INTERROTTA
    0 85670 560 8   £6.95

... 21 LEON BATTISTA ALBERTI
    0 85670 559 4   £6.95

... 22 HAWKSMOOR'S CHRISTCHURCH
    0 85670 650 7   £3.95

... 23 NEO-CLASSICISM
    0 85670 626 4   £6.95

... 24 BRITAIN IN THE 30s
    0 85670 627 2   £6.95

... 25 AALTO AND AFTER
    0 85670 701 5   £4.95

... 31 URBANITY
    0 85670 746 5   £6.95

... 33 BRITISH ARCHITECTS 1981
    0 85670 750 3   £6.95

... 34 ROMANTIC HOUSES
    0 85670 754 6   £4.95

... 37 ANGLO AMERICAN SUBURB
    0 85670 690 6   £6.95

... 38 CURRENT PROJECTS
    0 85670 768 6   £4.95

... 44 FOREST EDGE & BERLIN
    0 85670 789 9   £8.95

... 46 DOLLS' HOUSES
    0 85670 827 5   £8.95

... 47 THE RUSSIAN AVANT-GARDE
    0 85670 832 1   £8.95

... 49 ELEMENTS OF ARCHITECTURE
    0 85670 834 8   £8.95

... 51 URBANISM
    0 85670 843 7   **£8.95**

... 52 BRITISH ARCHITECTURE 1984
    0 85670 854 3   £8.95

... 53 BUILDING & RATIONAL ARCH
    0 85670 848 8   £8.95

... 54 LEON KRIER
RP/ND   0 85670 844 5   £8.95

... 55 IAKOV CHERNIKHOV
    0 85670 841 0   £8.95

... 56 UIA CAIRO INT. EXHIBITION
    0 85670 852 6   £8.95

... 57 AMERICAN ARCHITECTURE
    0 85670 855 0   £8.95

... 58 REVISION OF THE MODERN
    0 85670 861 5   £8.95

... 60 LE CORBUSIER ARCHIVE
    0 85670 696 5   £8.95

... 61 DESIGNING A HOUSE
    0 85670 888 7   £8.95

... 62 VIENNA DREAM AND REALITY
    0 85670 886 0   £8.95

... 4/86 MINARDI, ABK, SPEER
    0 85670 894 1   £3.95

... 6/86 KLOTZ, ROB KRIER, STIRLING,
    0 85670 902 6   £3.95

...7/86 TRADITION, INVENTION, CONVENTION
    0 85670 903 4   £3.95

... 9/86 AMERICAN URBANISM 1
    0 85670 905 0   £3.95

... 64 A HOUSE FOR TODAY
    0 85670 911 5   £8.95

... 66   NEOCLASSICAL ARCHITECTURE
    0 85670 887 9   £8.95

... 67 TRADITION & ARCHITECTURE
    0 85670 890 9   £8.95

... 68 SOVIET ARCHITECTURE
    0 85670 920 4   £8.95

... 69 ARCHITECTURE OF DEMOCRACY
    0 85670 923 9   £8.95

... 70 ENGINEERING & ARCHITECTURE
    0 85670 932 8   £8.95

... 72 DECONSTRUCTION IN ARCH
    0 85670 941 7   £8.95

... 73 JAPANESE ARCHITECTURE
RP/ND   0 85670 950 6   £8.95

... 74 CONTEMPORARY ARCH
    0 85670 953 0   £8.95

... 75 IMITATION & INNOVATION
    0 85670 954 9   £8.95

... 76 NEW DIRECTIONS IN ARCHITECTURE
    0 85670 992 1   £8.95

... 77 DECONSTRUCTION II
    0 85670 994 8   £8.95

... 78 DRAWING INTO ARCHITECTURE
    0 85670 997 2   £8.95

... 79 PRINCE CHARLES & ARCH. DEBATE
    1 85490 021 8   £8.95

... 80 CONSTRUCTIVISM & CHERNIKHOV
    1 85490 019 6   £8.95

... 81 RECONSTRUCTION/DECONSTRUCTION
    1 85490 000 5   £8.95

... 82 WEXNER CENTER: EISENMAN
    1 85490 027 7   £8.95

... 83 URBAN CONCEPTS
    1 85490 955 7   £8.95

... 84 NEW ARCHITECTURE
    1 85490 029 3   £8.95

... 85 JAMES STIRLING MICHAEL WILFORD
    1 85490 042 0   £8.95

... 86 THE NEW MODERN AESTHETIC
    1 85490 043 9   £8.95

... 87 DECONSTRUCTION III
    1 85490 050 1   £8.95

... 88 POST-MODERNISM ON TRIAL
    1 85490 044 7   £8.95

... 89 A NEW SPIRIT IN ARCHITECTURE
    1 85490 092 7   £8.95

... **A DECADE OF ARCHITECTURAL DESIGN**   1 85490 062 5   £35.00

Special Offer to Subscribers
until 31.8.91   **£29.50**

ART & DESIGN

1990 ANNUAL SUBSCRIPTION RATE (for six double issues inc p&p) *Art & Design*, UK only £39.50. Europe £45. Overseas US$75. Reduced Student Rate: UK £35. Europe £39.50. Overseas US$65. Subscriptions may be backdated to any issue.

... 1 BRITISH ART 20th CENTURY
    0 85670 912 3   £7.95

... 2 POST-MODERN OBJECT
    0 85670 914 X   £7.95

... 3 ABSTRACT ART
    0 85670 919 0   £7.95

... 4 THE POST-AVANT-GARDE
    0 85670 922 0   £7.95

... 5 BRITISH AND AMERICAN ART
    0 85670 930 1   £7.95

... 6 SCULPTURE TODAY
    0 85670 931 X   £7.95

... 7 DAVID HOCKNEY
    0 85670 935 2   £7.95

... 8 THE NEW MODERNISM
    0 85670 940 9   £7.95

... 9 THE CLASSICAL SENSIBILITY
    0 85670 948 4   £7.95

... 10 ART IN THE AGE OF PLURALISM
    0 85670 957 3   £7.95

... 11 BRITISH ART NOW
    0 85670 958 1   £7.95

... 12 THE NEW ROMANTICS
    0 85670 956 5   £7.95

... 13 ITALIAN ART NOW
    0 85670 993 X   £7.95

... 14 40 UNDER 40
    0 85670 995 6   £7.95

... 15 MALEVICH
    0 85670 998 0   £7.95

... 16 NEW YORK NEW ART
    1 85490 004 8   £7.95

... 17 GERMAN ART NOW
    1 85490 023 4   £7.95

... 18 ASPECTS OF MODERN ART
    1 85490 020 X   £7.95

... 19 NEW ART INTERNATIONAL
    1 85490 018 8   £7.95

... 20 ART & THE TECTONIC
    1 85490 037 4   £7.95

... 21 ART MEETS SCIENCE & SPIRITUALITY
    1 85490 038 2   £8.95

ARCHITECTURAL MONOGRAPHS

SUBSCRIPTION RATES (for four issues inc p&p, publication irregular) *Architectural Monographs*, UK only £49.50. Europe £59.50. Overseas US$99.50. Reduced Student Rate: UK £45. Europe £55. Overseas US$89.50. Subscriptions may be backdated to any issue.

... 4 ALVAR AALTO
    0 85670 421 0   PB£14.95

... 6 EDWIN LUTYENS Rev Edn
    0 85670 422 9   PB£14.95

... 8 JOHN SOANE
    0 85670 805 4   PB£14.95

... 9 TERRY FARRELL
    0 85670 842 9   PB£14.95

... 10 RICHARD ROGERS
    0 85670 786 4   PB£14.95

... 11 MIES VAN DER ROHE
    0 85670 685 X   PB£14.95

... 12 LE CORBUSIER: Early Work
    0 85670 804 6   PB£14.95

... 13 HASSAN FATHY
    0 85670 918 2   PB£14.95

... 14 TADAO ANDO
    1 85490 007 2   PB£14.95

... 15 AHRENDS BURTON & KORALEK
    0 85670 927 1   PB£14.95

... 16 ROBERT STERN
NYP/91   1 85490 008 0   PB£14.95

... 17 DANIEL LIBESKIND
NYP/91   1 85490 097 8   PB£14.95

... 18 VENTURI SCOTT BROWN
NYP/91   1 85490 098 6   PB£14.95

... C F A VOYSEY
NYP/91   1 85490 032 3   PB£14.95

UIA JOURNAL

Published in cooperation with the International Union of Architects. SUBSCRIPTION RATES (for four issues inc p&p, publication irregular) *UIA Journal*, UK and Europe £49.50. Overseas US$89.50. Reduced Student Rate: UK and Europe £45. Overseas US$79.50.

... 1 VISION OF THE MODERN
RP/ND   0 85670 915 8   £12.95

... 2 DECONSTRUCTION – A STUDENT GUIDE
    1 85490 034 X   £12.95

JOURNAL OF PHILOSOPHY AND THE VISUAL ARTS

SUBSCRIPTION RATES (for four issues inc p&p, publication irregular) *Journal of Philosophy and the Visual Arts*, UK only £45. Europe £55. Overseas US$89.50. Reduced Student Rate: UK £39.50. Europe £49.50. Overseas US$89.50.

... PHILOSOPHY & THE VISUAL ARTS
    0 85670 966 2   £12.95

... PHILOSOPHY & ARCHITECTURE
    1 85490 016 1   £12.95

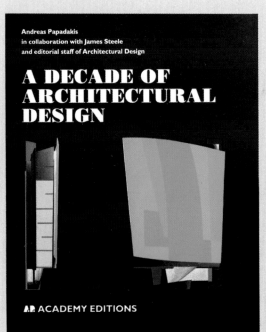

Geoffrey Broadbent
DECONSTRUCTION
A STUDENT GUIDE

UIA
Journal of Architectural Theory and Criticism 1:2:91

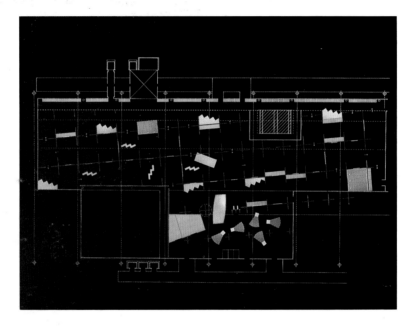

Specially for students, this guide, written by Professor Geoffrey Broadbent of Portsmouth School of Architecture, analyses the philosophical and linguistic theories of Deconstruction showing the development of Structuralism through to Derridean Deconstruction and then exploring its implications on realised projects today.

The volume covers the subject in three parts. Firstly, in the 'Architecture of Deconstruction', Geoffrey Broadbent traces the rise of Deconstruction in architecture, showing how theories have been taken on board by architects in recent years. In the 'Philosophy of Deconstruction', philosophical and linguistic theories are analysed from the development of Structuralism through to Derridean Deconstruction. Finally, the third section looks at 'Deconstruction in Action', giving a concise but broad overview of a variety of architects' work, including interviews with three of the major proponents of Deconstruction: Bernard Tschumi, Zaha Hadid and Coop Himmelblau.

96 pages, over 50 illustrations, paperback £12.95 (by post add £3)
ISBN: 1 85490 035 8
Available from good bookstores worldwide

Published by

ACADEMY EDITIONS • LONDON
7 Holland Street London W8 4AN Tel: 071-402 2141